THE ULTIMATE
CHAMPION

THE ULTIMATE
CHAMPION

A Life Experiencing God's Presence,
God's Favor, and God's Promotion

JOHN JACOBS

THOMAS NELSON PUBLISHERS®
Nashville

Published in Nashville, Tennessee, by Thomas Nelson, Inc.

Library of Congress Cataloging-in-Publication Data

Jacobs, John, 1959-
     The ultimate champion : a life experiencing God's presence,
   God's favor, and God's promotion / John Jacobs.
       p.   cm.
     ISBN 0-7852-6916-9 (pbk.)
     1. Christian life. I. Title.
     BV4501.2.J31362000
     248.4—dc21   99-054685
                                                                          CIP

Printed in the United States of America

1 2 3 4 5 6 QPV 05 04 03 02 01 00

This book is dedicated to my mother, Paula Jacobs, who was an expert at telling me what I could become. She taught me that people will rise to the level you expect them to. She always expected me to rise to the top.

My mom was a teacher who firmly believed in the power of positive reinforcement. She could take a student no one else could handle and challenge that student to become the person he or she was capable of becoming. She told me of the potential that God had for me, and I will always be grateful to her for that. Throughout my life she has reminded me of the call God had for me and the greatness He put inside me. With sincere respect and admiration for your goodness and for everything you taught me, thank you, Mom!

CONTENTS

CONTENTS

FOREWORD

Scripture is very clear that God finds pleasure in being involved with our lives. It even says that God can be motivated to promote our lives based on how we respond to Him. First Peter 5:6 (NKJV) says, "Therefore humble yourselves under the mighty hand of God, that He may exalt you in due time."

If you apply certain biblical principles to your life, God can do more with you in five minutes than you can do in fifty years, even if you work hard. Proverbs 16:3 (NIV) tells us, "Commit to the Lord whatever you do, and your plans will succeed." Furthermore, Psalm 37:4 (NKJV) says, "Delight yourself . . . in the LORD, and He shall give you the desires of your heart."

When you are a child of God, people do not hold your future—God does. Psalm 75:6 (TLB) states, "promotion and power come from nowhere on earth, but only from God." If you are willing to surrender your abilities to God and use your gifts and talents for Him, God's response is a highly motivated one: He will do great things with your life.

The Ultimate Champion is not just someone who has excelled in a sport, a career, or a profession but also someone who sees things as God sees them. The Ultimate Champion does what he can with what he has, where he is, to the glory of God. The surprise is, God will increase what this person has, and He will never leave that person where he is. Because the Ultimate Champion experiences God's presence, His favor, and His promotion, that person is able to triumph over insurmountable odds (Psalm 37:23–24).

A prerequisite to becoming a champion is having a coach who is willing to put you in the game, promote you to the starting team, and give you "the big break." This is also true of the game of life. The Bible says that when you surrender to God to make a difference for Him, your life is "hidden with Christ" (Col. 3:3). When God promotes a person, no one can stop that person. Indeed, Revelation 2:26 (TLB) says, "To every one who overcomes—who to the very end keeps on doing things that please me—I will give power over the nations."

The greatest champion—the Ultimate Champion—is not the person who has won a Super Bowl ring, an Olympic medal, or some other worldly prize, but the person who has surrendered and submitted himself to God. The Ultimate Champion makes a difference for God by touching other people's lives. As a result, the Ultimate Champion feels God's presence, His favor, and His promotion.

Do What You Can with What You Have

Every cell in my body surged with adrenaline when a prison official announced over the intercom: "All men who want to see John Jacobs, who is second in the nation in weight lifting, break a pair of police handcuffs and blow up a hot-water bottle, meet in the prison field."

As a young college student, I conducted a prison Bible study for about fifteen men on normal weekends. On this particular Saturday I decided to take a big risk and invite the entire prison to watch me break a pair of handcuffs. (I had only done this a few times while practicing privately.) I entered the prison complex with my Bible, a hot-water bottle, and a new pair of regulation police handcuffs.

To my surprise, the entire prison population showed up! Seven hundred inmates filed onto the exercise field. Every one of those young men had felt the cold bite of handcuffs around their wrists. I had their complete attention.

"We are saved by grace through faith," I explained. "And not through our own abilities or good deeds. Salvation is a free gift because Jesus purchased your pardon from an 'eternal prison' called hell. Jesus may not take you out of this prison, but He will take the prison out of you!"

That day *seven hundred* prison inmates raised their hands to receive Christ!

My experience at the prison that day proved to me that amazing things happen when you live each day in God's favor, things that simply cannot be explained or duplicated by mere human effort or ingenuity. Since God can do more in five minutes than I can do in fifty years, I am convinced that nothing is more exciting than experiencing life with the favor of God. The problem is, most people don't know what God's favor is or how to release it in their lives.

We can learn a great deal about God's favor from His Word and from practical examples of divine favor in human experience. I can tell you that when God puts His touch on your life, things will seem to go right for you. Yes, you will still face obstacles and trials, and you may even fail from time to time. Yet, at key points in your life, you will also experience "divine appointments" with people who want to help you for no apparent reason or personal benefit.

More than two decades ago, Paul and Jan Crouch invited me to appear on their show on the Trinity Broadcasting Network. I broke a pair of handcuffs and then explained to the Crouches and their television audience the outreach ministry of my select group of world-class athletes called the Power Team. The Crouches took a personal interest in me (another example of God's favor at work), and they asked the Power Team to host our own television program. TBN videotaped some of our crusades and aired them during our program. After a year of national exposure on TBN, we held our first citywide crusade in Tulsa, Oklahoma. In five nights, sixty-three thousand people attended the meetings, and seven thousand people accepted Jesus.

RUSSIA RECEIVES JESUS

During the last year before the communist regime fell from power, we conducted seven televised crusades in Russia. An estimated one hundred million Russian viewers watched as we presented the gospel of Jesus Christ. This happened before the fall of the Berlin Wall. Since then, the Power Team has ministered around the world and throughout the United States. As I write this, we are opening new Power Team ministry offices in five countries.

Thirty-two Power Team members working in eight teams ministered in more than one thousand schools in 1999. In the first twenty-one years of our ministry, several million people walked forward to receive Christ as their Savior. In 1998 alone, God allowed us to lead more than one hundred thousand people to Christ, and even more came to Him in 1999. That was the year Chuck Norris featured the Power Team in a powerful episode of his prime-time television show *Walker, Texas Ranger*. The demand for our ministry in high schools, middle schools, and churches is greater than ever in the wake of the violence that erupted at Columbine High School in Colorado and in other schools across America in recent years.

Every day I say, "Lord, what is going to happen next?" Can we attribute the Power Team's success to my personal talents, ministry contacts, personal knowledge, or know-how? Absolutely not. People often ask me, "John, how in the world can someone who breaks bricks, splinters boards, snaps handcuffs, and blows up hot-water bottles get to do what you've done?" Without exception I tell them, "It is *God's favor.*"

God's favor will elevate you to new levels of influence due to no special accomplishment or virtue of your own. He will even promote your children or other family members. If you notice that you seem to be at the right place at the right time, if even the busy affairs of this world seem to work to your benefit, then God's favor is at work in your life.

One of the clearest examples of God's favor is found in a remarkable story recorded in the gospel of Mark. I like to claim this story as my own life story:

> While he[Jesus] was in Bethany, reclining at the table in the home of a man known as Simon the Leper, a woman came with an alabaster jar of very expensive perfume, made of pure nard. She broke the jar and poured the perfume on his head.
>
> Some of those present were saying indignantly to one another, "Why this waste of perfume? It could have been sold for more than a year's wages and the money given to the poor." And they rebuked her harshly.
>
> "Leave her alone," said Jesus. "Why are you bothering her? She has done a beautiful thing to me. The poor you will always have with you, and you can help them any time you want. But you will not always have me." (Mark 14:3–7)

I'M GOING TO BRAG ON YOU FOREVER

How did this woman who anointed Jesus manage to motivate Him so much that He personally shut the mouths of her critics? Whatever she did, Jesus was so moved and motivated by her actions that He instantly rose to her defense. The Son of God personally rebuked those who complained and countered every religious argument they leveled against her. Then Jesus revealed a great truth and promised something to her that should catch our attention!

"She did what she could. She poured perfume on my body beforehand to prepare for my burial. I tell you the truth, wherever the gospel is preached throughout the world, what she has done will also be told, in memory of her." (Mark 14:8–9)

What causes this kind of response from God? The key wasn't really the bottle of perfume; it was what it represented. Jesus said, "She did what she could." He also announced that this woman would receive worldwide honor and would be remembered forever. He said it right in front of the nationally recognized religious leaders who had condemned her. In essence Jesus was saying, "I'm going to brag on you forever."

THE SECRET THAT MOVES GOD'S HEART

Although I have searched and studied the Scriptures for decades, I can't find this kind of response anywhere else in the New Testament. This story in Mark 14 reveals a secret that moves the heart of God! The good news is that you, too, can receive the same response from God if you do what this woman did. This is the first of twelve biblical keys that will help you fulfill your destiny and become the Ultimate Champion:

If you do what you can, with what you have, right where you are, then God will increase what you have, and He won't leave you where you are.

If you are willing to apply this key principle in your life, you will see God's favor as you have never seen it before. God will "turn on the spout where the glory comes out," and His favor will fall upon your family and cover your children. I challenge you to apply this principle in your life.

God has given everyone certain gifts and talents, and I promise you that He has made a costly investment in you. When you are willing to invest your life, your gifts, and your talents to build His kingdom and further His work, God sees your willingness as an expression of commitment and devotion. When you do what you can with what you have, the Bible teaches that you are motivating God to act on your behalf.

We can't "earn" salvation or eternal life with God—Jesus already did that for us on the cross. However, we can please Him by demonstrating our faith and doing something with what we have to build His kingdom. In turn, He delights in responding to us in many different ways.

JESUS SAID,
"YOU WILL BE ONE OF MY HEROES"

The Son of God essentially told the woman in Mark 14, "Wherever the Bible is preached, you are going to be one of My heroes of faith. I'm going to tell your story. I'm going to brag on you forever." I think you will agree that this is the pinnacle of success.

Do you want to be one of God's heroes? Do you want your life story to be one of His stories? Would you like to hear God brag on you forever? That is as good as it gets.

What did this woman really do? Did she preach crusades all over the world? No. Did she build millions of churches? No. Did she work great miracles? No. What did she do? Let me repeat once again what Jesus said about this woman in Mark 14:8: "*She did what she could.*"

When we do what we can with what we have for God's sake, He is moved. When the God of heaven gets moved, nothing can stop Him. When God promotes somebody, nothing and no one can stop it. The critics can't stop it, and lack of opportunity can't stop it. When God promotes someone, that settles it, because God gets what He wants. I'm not making this up. The Bible says:

> In his heart a man plans his course, but the LORD determines his steps. (Prov. 16:9)

> No one from the east or the west or from the desert can exalt [or promote] a man. But it is God who judges: He brings one down, he exalts another. (Ps. 75:6–7)

> Delight yourself in the LORD and he will give you the desires of your heart. (Ps. 37:4)

> Commit to the LORD whatever you do, and your plans will succeed. (Prov. 16:3)

These Scripture passages strongly imply that God's favor is really an expression of God's promotion. It is an expression of His pleasure being poured out upon us. His favor falls upon us regardless of the circumstances we are going through at any given time. God delights in fulfilling our dreams and promoting His people in unprecedented ways.

I am not giving you some manipulation technique. This is a Bible-based principle that God loves to honor, and it bears repeating: *If you do what you can with what you have, right where you are, then God will increase what you have, and He won't leave you where you are.* Every time you dare to obey God and do what you can with what you have, heaven gets bigger, and hell gets smaller.

THEY DID WHAT THEY COULD

Many people don't know that my parents were divorced when I was in grade school. I went through middle school and high school without my father's presence. Yet God favored me by sending other people into my life to do what they could.

After the divorce, I moved with my mother and sister to Evansville, Indiana, to be with my grandparents. My grandparents constantly demonstrated the joy of the Lord in their lives, and the favor of God was upon them. My grandfather served as the head deacon at their church, and my grandmother was in charge of the senior citizens meeting. It was my grandparents who took me to church for the first time.

My grandfather taught math in high school for forty years, and he also taught night school three days a week until he reached his seventies. He finally stopped substitute teaching when he turned seventy-seven. One of his church duties was to keep the Sunday school records for the two thousand people who attended his church. He spent three hours every Sunday afternoon diligently totaling the attendance and offering records. To a seventeen-year-old, that was the most boring thing you could do.

One Sunday I walked into the living room and asked, "Granddad, why do you sit here every Sunday afternoon for two or three hours and total up all of those Sunday school records? Isn't it boring?"

He looked at me and said something that I will never forget: "John, I've been a math teacher for forty years, *and this is what I can do for God.*" He was saying the same thing that the woman who anointed Jesus would have said: "This is my bottle of perfume, and I am going to pour it on Jesus' head." My grandfather did what he could with what he had.

When my family first moved from Louisiana to Indiana, we didn't live with my grandparents. For the first six months, we lived in a little apartment in a rough neighborhood where gangs often beat me up. My grandparents felt they had to do something, so they spent all of their savings to buy a nice, big house directly across the street from the church. We all moved in together.

My grandparents' investment made a difference in my life. They offered what they could, and by God's grace, it was enough to change the course of my life. I began to attend church faithfully at Bethel Temple along with the rest of my family. My mom, sister, and I even taught Sunday school there.

Other key people came into my life as well. A science teacher named Dan Twill, who was a real "man's man," took me under his wing and taught me how to hunt and fish. A few years later, the youth pastor at Bethel Temple in Evansville also played a key role in my life as a mentor and friend. (At this writing, he is still faithfully ministering to the youth at Bethel Temple.)

IF YOU CAN'T SING GOOD, SING LOUD!

I couldn't always bench-press six hundred pounds or roll up two frying pans like tortillas. When I turned sixteen I wanted to do something for God in my church. I am convinced that this is one of the proofs that you are saved: You should *want* to do something for God.

I figured that one way to serve God was to try out for the youth choir. My mom's first response was: "Honey, please don't—you are tone-deaf." One of my buddies was a bit more positive. He said, "Hey, John, if you can't sing good, sing loud!"

So I did. I sang *really* loud. After two weeks I showed up on Wednesday night for practice, and no one was there. In fact, no one would even tell me where they practiced! My mom was right. I was weeded out of the youth choir. I didn't stop though. I was determined to find something I *could* do for God, and I found it.

Our church had a special ministry for mentally handicapped people who were thirty to fifty years old. I knew that God loved these precious people just as much as He loved me. So, I began to ride along on the buses to help pick them up. I also helped minister in services especially designed for them.

You see, I found something I could do in my church. I believe God wants every Christian to be involved in some way in his or her local church. He gave each of us unique gifts and talents that He expects us to use for His glory.

The youth pastor took me under his wing during the three years I worked with the mentally handicapped and really encouraged me. I was very involved in the youth group, especially in outreach work, where we tried to help young people who weren't directly involved in our church. This was when I began to realize that I really had a heart to reach the unreachable.

THE KING OF THE PIT MEETS THE ROWDY STONER

When I was in high school, I would do anything I could to influence other teenagers for the Lord. I helped start a prayer meeting at Harrison High School and was deeply involved in football and wrestling. My physical size and strength levels began to increase dramatically during my junior year, when my weight increased from 185 to 225 pounds. In my senior year I shot up to a height of six feet, three inches, and my weight increased to 260 pounds.

Training in a gym called "The Pit" under the direction of a weight-lifting coach named Dick Conners, I placed second in the National Teenage Power Lifting Championships that year. Wherever I trained—whether it was at The Pit, in the high school weight room, or at the local YMCA—I quickly noticed that when I did some kind of exceptional lift, it would capture people's attention. This gave me a perfect opportunity to share the Lord, pray with people, or simply encourage them. This revelation was significant because I knew that a lot of these people wouldn't have listened to anyone else. People are fascinated by strength.

Roger was a rowdy "stoner," a rough, tough, and wild guy

involved in drugs.[1] He wore camouflage clothes to school and smelled of marijuana. (The typical church kid would have walked away and said, "Don't mess with this guy." However, God had prepared me to reach out to people like Roger.)

One day in 1976, Roger walked through the high school weight room, and I saw my chance. I politely cornered him. "Hey, Jesus can take care of your problems. The Lord cares about you. Why don't you go to youth group with me?" I took him to youth group that night, and he gave his heart to the Lord. God so drastically changed Roger that he went from making straight F's to making straight A's his junior year. It caused such a commotion in our school that his teachers even asked him to tell their classes what had happened to him.

Roger shared with me that his family was deeply involved in the occult. He said they often played with Ouija boards and conducted seances. They even saw hooded figures walking around their home. Roger and I began to pray for his family. About a month later, his mom and three sisters walked into the church, and all were saved. Roger was a perfect example of 2 Corinthians 5:17: "If anyone is in Christ, he is a new creation." God totally changed Roger's heart and life. He went from being the local school dope dealer to becoming the local school hope dealer! We became good friends and worked together in the morning prayer meeting at our school.

WRESTLING A GIANT

Evansville's Bossey High School was our rough, crosstown rival. An African-American football player and wrestler there, whom I will call Jeffrey, was known as the toughest of the tough. He had actually broken a rival's neck during a high school football game. He was feared for good reason. I had to wrestle Jeffrey during my junior year. He was eighteen but physically looked as if he were twenty-five, with massive biceps and an attitude to match. I felt like a kid wrestling a giant.

I was winning the match, however, until the third period when I made a mistake and Jeffrey pinned me. Secretly, I was glad that I had overcome my fear of him and had done so well in the match. That was when I began to pray for Jeffrey.

When Bethel Temple sponsored a Paul Anderson crusade, it drew in a lot of the athletes from our town. Mr. Anderson was a former Olympic medalist who had set world records as a power lifter. He used to lift Volkswagen cars and other massive objects in public demonstrations. I helped with his crusade at Bethel Temple, and I will never forget the night Jeffrey walked forward to receive Christ.

I counseled Jeffrey afterward and told him about the parable of the sower (Matt. 13:1–13; Mark 4:1–9). I said, "Now you have to let your heart be fertile ground and be nurtured." He started going to our church occasionally. We became friends.

During my senior year of high school, the church brought in an evangelist who did martial arts demonstrations that drew in more of my tough friends from high school. He placed a watermelon on someone's chest and cut it in half with a sword. He performed a number of classic karate feats to draw people in before he preached the gospel. When my tough friends went forward and accepted the Lord, I thought, *Man, what a great ministry tool.* The evangelist and I became friends, and that summer I worked as a counselor at his youth camp.

SWALLOWING A GOLDFISH IN SUNDAY SCHOOL

While all of this was going on, I continued to work with the mentally handicapped at my church. After three years, the pastor asked me if I would like to teach Sunday school.

I said, "Sure, I'll do what I can." He took me at my word and assigned me to teach a class for ten high school students. They had already gone through five teachers in six months, so it was no easy task. It didn't matter though. I did what I could and worked hard. Within a month we were up to thirty students.

But I wanted to reach even more students. When I won a goldfish in a contest at a fall festival, I remembered an article I'd just read in *Life* magazine about the 1950s fad of swallowing goldfish. I took my goldfish to Sunday school and told the young people in my class, "If we have two hundred in this class in one month, I will swallow this goldfish live!" Now, I thought I was safe with the impossible number of two hundred, but I've learned that you are never safe when it comes to teenagers wanting to see something gross!

One month later, I counted two hundred thirty-eight people in my class. I held up the goldfish bowl and thought, *Oh, man, this is really going to happen.* Every eye was on me as I scooped up the goldfish and dangled it over my mouth. *I'll kind of squeeze it first,* I thought. *Maybe it will die, and no one will know.*

When I started to squeeze the goldfish, it popped right out of my fingers. I managed to catch it with my other hand. In a panic, I grabbed a glass of water, threw the fish in my mouth, and gulped down the water. I didn't know then that you should never, ever drink water while swallowing a goldfish because it causes the fish to get stuck in your throat, and it helps the fish live longer. The magazine article said to drink Coke, but I hadn't read far enough. It was an experience I never hope to repeat. It is safe to say that my first "feat of strength" (squeezing the goldfish) was a flop.

The good news is that although the goldfish lost its life, thirty high school students received Christ and were saved that day. That sounds silly, but it is important for you to understand my heart. I wanted to do whatever I could to reach people for God, to serve my church, and to be involved for the kingdom of God.

The summer after my graduation from high school, I saw Mr. Universe blow up a hot-water bottle on television. This gave me some ideas of my own. I had taken some karate and started breaking bricks. When I thought about the karate demonstrations and the hot-water bottle feat, I realized those things could be great tools for our youth group.

I performed public feats of strength for the first time in 1978 for our youth group at Bethel Temple. I broke a big block of ice and a stack of bricks with my arm. I also blew up a hot-water bottle before I preached. It wasn't much by current Power Team standards, but it was a beginning.

In the summer of 1978, I contacted my high school friends Roger (who had become a football star in his senior year after he received Christ and got off drugs) and Jeffrey. I said, "Look, guys, why don't we each do a feat of strength and minister?" Some girls from our youth group formed a singing group to complement our power feats program. We conducted fifteen crusades in the Midwest that summer. We each did feats of strength, someone would give a testimony, and then I would preach. That is where the Power Team concept began.

A BIBLE TEACHER IN THE PRISON

The next year I went to Oral Roberts University in Tulsa, Oklahoma, where I remember praying, "God, here is my life. Use it for something great. I want to win people to You, Lord; I want to make a difference for You." That was when I began leading the Bible study for prison inmates on weekends.

One day a detective I'd met at church told me, "John, as strong as you are, you could break a pair of my handcuffs." I didn't believe it, but he insisted that I could. He began to work with me. Before long I snapped my first pair of handcuffs! (I don't know how many sets of handcuffs I've gone through since then—somewhere in the thousands.) One week later, I snapped a pair of handcuffs and blew up a hot-water bottle in front of the seven hundred prisoners I mentioned earlier.

I rushed back to my dorm room to tell my roommate, "You won't believe it! I broke the handcuffs, blew up the hot-water bottle, and preached to seven hundred men—and then they *all* got saved!" My roommate competed in decathlons, a track and field event consisting of ten grueling contests. He picked up a thick city phone book and said, "Watch what I can do," and then he ripped it into two pieces. I said, "Cool. Come with me to the prison next Saturday to rip your phone book and give your testimony. I'll break another pair of handcuffs." We ended up holding seventeen prison revivals that summer. I remember selling my spare tire just to make it to one of those revivals.

JESUS WOULD NEVER BEND BARS WITH HIS TEETH

After three years at ORU, I transferred to a denominational Bible college in Florida and began to attend the First Assembly of God, now known as Carpenter's Home Church, pastored by Karl Strader. I continued to do the Power Team and helped out at the church, but I soon realized that not everyone was so excited about my unusual ministry methods. Oral Roberts University was a progressive and innovative university, but the denominational Bible college I attended in Florida saw things very differently at that time.

I was criticized and put down by professors and students alike. I was told that bending bars with my teeth was ridiculous, and that doing feats of strength was not the right way to present the gospel of Christ. Half of the teachers tried to talk me out of doing the power feats. Others said, "Well, if you do the feats, at least make sure you put on your tie before you preach." (Honestly, I think *Jesus* would bend bars with His teeth if it would bring one more person into the kingdom of God.)

All I knew was that when I performed feats of strength, crowds came, and sinners were saved. I made up my mind that I wasn't going to let anybody talk me out of what God had planned for me. Although I had maintained a 3.5 to 3.7 grade point average at ORU, I almost flunked out of the denominational Bible school because I missed some classes while conducting outreach crusades. Every time I missed a day, the professors would mark me down a letter grade.

I thank God that no document or college held the key to my future. Only God did. I knew that if I focused on what He had for me, then He would promote me. I have always had places to preach or hold crusades.

I managed to graduate from Bible college after all, and I began to conduct Power Team crusades full-time. At first churches were slow to accept the Power Team, but within six months the word began to get out.

FISHING WITH BRICKS, BOARDS, STEEL BARS, AND PLENTY OF ICE

Before long I was preaching in the largest churches in America in all kinds of denominations, simply because I did what I could with what I had. Some people have rejected my ministry, saying, "Breaking bricks, lifting weights, blowing up hot-water bottles, and snapping handcuffs isn't my thing." I always tell them, "Those things are only *the bait*."

When my wife and I go fishing, she doesn't like to handle the bait. I have to bait her hook with minnows or worms. Once she gets a fish on that line, I can forget about helping her. She is quick to tell me, "No, no—I can do it!" Why? Because she is excited about the catch, not the bait.

The bait should never be our focus. As born-again Christians, we have to be in love with catching fish! We don't conduct Power Team crusades because we love the bait; we do it because we love to draw people to Christ.

MA'AM, IT'S ALL THE SAME TO GOD

I'll never forget the church crusade where I met some elderly women in the lobby who made coffee, shook hands, and greeted people before each meeting. One beautiful lady shook my hand and recited an encouraging Scripture verse. I replied, "Ma'am, this is a wonderful ministry you have as you greet people on behalf of the church."

She shook her head and told me, "Oh, it is nothing like yours. You reach millions of people for Jesus." In that moment, God put it in my heart to tell her, "Ma'am, it is all the same to God." You see, God does not compare us or measure us against other people. We aren't competing for His favor. God is concerned about one thing: Will you *do what you can with what you have, right where you are* for Him? That precious woman tapped the very heartbeat of God through her humble service in Jesus' name. Her ministry was a practical demonstration of what it means to "pour your bottle of perfume on Jesus' head."

If I've learned one thing in this life, it is this: If you do what you can with what you have where you are, God will increase what you have, and He won't leave you where you are. I have met one person who seems to exemplify this godly principle more than anyone else.

PLAYING GUITAR WITH HIS TOES

My wife, Ruthanne, and I met Tony when he performed as a special guest on our TBN television program. Tony plays the guitar with his toes because he was born without arms. This born-again

Catholic is making a worldwide impact for God. He is known and loved by the pope, by countless world leaders, and by Christian leaders from numerous denominations, and his life story has inspired several books and a movie.

All Tony does is sit on a stool, play his guitar with his toes, and sing love songs about Jesus with a big smile. When I said, "Tony, you're having a world impact for God," he told me, "*I'm just doing what I can with what I have for God. He is promoting me.*"

Can you imagine how Tony's mother must have felt when the doctors held up her newborn baby? What if the nurse had said, "Someday he's going to have a world impact for God playing the guitar"? Everyone in the room would have thought, *What a sick joke.* Many doctors in our pro-abortion era would have conducted an ultrasound exam during her pregnancy and warned Tony's mother that her fetus was deformed. Their advice may have been, "It would be better to abort this baby."

It is true that Tony has only part of a body to offer God. However, when he used what he had for God's glory, then God gave him worldwide influence, which has brought him before kings and presidents. I know God will do the same for you because He did it for me.

I believe miracles will happen when you do what you can with what you have to honor God. By the time I was twenty-five, I was preaching in the largest churches in America—now this is the same person who was kicked out of youth choir and swallowed a goldfish to impress high school kids. That is evidence of God's favor, and it begins when you do what you can with what you have to serve God.

Turn to God with Your Whole Heart and Find Your Destiny

Janet was a teenage prostitute who worked the streets of Beverly Hills, California.[1] She never "planned" to become a prostitute, and she probably knew that she was born for a higher purpose than that. Janet was trapped in a life that was the opposite of what God always intended for her. She left home and ultimately became addicted to drugs. If anyone dared to witness to her, she would only spit in the person's face and boldly tell him or her that she was a satanist.

Shortly after the Power Team first went on nationwide television about fifteen years ago, Janet was watching television and snorting cocaine with twenty of her friends when she accidentally turned the channel to TBN. She tuned in just as I began to break a pair of handcuffs. Since everyone in the room had been handcuffed by the police at one time or another, the idea of watching someone snap some police handcuffs really appealed to them.

When I broke the handcuffs, some of Janet's friends even cheered. The group listened to me preach about Jesus for about one minute before they turned the channel. God used that brief moment to plant an eternal seed in Janet. She never forgot what she saw on television that night.

The next time the Power Team came to Los Angeles, Janet saw an advertisement and decided to attend the crusade. That very night she came forward and received Jesus Christ as her Savior and Lord.

Janet turned to the Lord with her whole heart, determined to totally change her lifestyle and follow Jesus. She went through rehabilitation at a Christian institution, and according to the latest reports, she is training to go on the mission field to fulfill her true destiny. Janet's story is an example of how God's power is revealed and released in response to total commitment. Her story illustrates the second key principle for becoming the Ultimate Champion:

Turn to God with your whole heart
and find your destiny.

SEEKING A CAUSE WORTH DYING FOR

Christians and non-Christians alike are concerned about their "destiny," or purpose for living. People across America are leaving high-paying executive jobs in search of a sense of significance. Some may leave their career positions to join the FBI, while others abandon their executive offices to help Greenpeace save the whales or to help preservation groups protect countless endangered species from civilization.

What causes skilled office workers to leave their comfortable beds in suburbia so they can block the path of massive logging trucks with their own bodies? They seek a cause worth dying for. By committing everything to the preservation of America's forest lands, they hope to find meaning for their lives.

More than anything else, this flight from the ivory towers of commerce and the traditional workplace is an outward symptom of an inward work of God. People from every walk of life are sensing a God-given hunger for their divine destiny, and nothing in their busy lives is satisfying their longing. True significance comes from God when we surrender everything to Jesus and commit our God-given abilities to Him for His purposes.

Some people witness to non-Christians by telling them, "You should be afraid of going to hell." I've discovered something that many people fear even more in *this life:* They are afraid of missing their destiny. They fear they won't fulfill the purpose for which they were born—and with good reason.

If you are a born-again Christian, you should have no fear of hell. However, you should be very concerned about fulfilling your destiny in Christ. Your only alternative may be spending eternity filled with regret because you chose to do nothing instead of fulfilling your eternal destiny.

CAN YOU AFFORD TO MISS YOUR DESTINY?

God created you as a unique person with a special, one-of-a-kind plan for your life. No one on this planet has ever been or ever will be exactly like you, even if you are an identical twin. God has decreed a destiny for you that can be fulfilled by only one person: you. Yes, God will do what must be done to see His will completed should you fail, but no one will fulfill your destiny just like you. Do you think that you can afford to miss the destiny God has for your life?

People who find and actively pursue their destiny tend to exhibit four biblical characteristics that are found in the life story of Josiah. This obscure king of Judah was descended from some of Judah's most sinful kings. His amazing story is found in the book of Second Kings:

Josiah was eight years old when he became king, and he reigned in Jerusalem thirty-one years. His mother's name was Jedidah daughter of Adaiah; she was from Bozkath. He did what was right in the eyes of the LORD and walked in all the ways of his father David, not turning aside to the right or to the left. (2 Kings 22:1–2)

Josiah's father, King Amon, was a wicked king who followed in the footsteps of his own father, King Manasseh. Manasseh was so evil that he even sacrificed one of his own sons in the fire to Baal.

Josiah was only eight years old when court officials assassinated his father, King Amon, only two years into his reign. The people of Judah put King Amon's killers to death and named young Josiah as their new king. Josiah inherited a nation filled with idolatry, immorality, and perversion (this description reminds me of modern-day America). The people of Judah didn't even have a copy of the Jewish Scriptures, the Old Testament. All that remained from the days when King David and King Solomon worshiped God was an abandoned and damaged temple.

The Bible tells us Josiah "did what was right in the eyes of the LORD" and walked in the ways "of his father [or ancestor] David," which means he lived a good, moral life. Yet, it appears that young Josiah wasn't satisfied with just being a good king. He sensed there was something *more* for him to do, but he didn't know what it was until he had ruled Judah for eighteen years.

After three generations of neglect, misuse, and abuse, the temple of God was in serious need of repair. In his eighteenth year as king, Josiah ordered the high priest to gather all of the money donated to repair the temple and to start the work. The high priest discovered something in the process—either in a dusty forgotten corner among some records or under the rubble and debris of a damaged area of the temple—that would transform King Josiah's life:

> Hilkiah the high priest said to Shaphan the secretary, "I have found the Book of the Law in the temple of the LORD." He gave it to Shaphan, who read it . . .
>
> Then Shaphan the secretary informed the king, "Hilkiah the priest has given me a book." And Shaphan read from it in the presence of the king. (2 Kings 22:8, 10)

Hilkiah brought King Josiah's chief court official the "Book of the Law" (probably the book of Deuteronomy)², and the king was eager to hear God's Word. This book was also called "the book of the covenant" because it described the blessing and cursing God pronounced on Abraham and his descendants as a part of His eternal covenant (2 Kings 23:2). Notice what happened when King Josiah heard the Scriptures read for the very first time: "When the king heard the words of the Book of the Law, *he tore his robes*" (2 Kings 22:11, italics mine).

The Word of God permanently changed the course of this young king's life. Three rebellious kings had preceded Josiah, so it was unlikely that any king of Judah in living memory had torn his clothes! King Josiah's heart was broken by what he heard because it was clear to him that Judah had turned away from the true God to worship false gods. He immediately tore his kingly robes and probably stood there shaking, totally overcome by emotion. Then King Josiah ordered the four men who were closest to him to ask the Lord what was meant by the words in the Book of the Law. Only a few people could hear God's voice in those days, so the men went straight to a godly woman named Huldah.

Huldah was married to the grandson of the royal tailor, and

23

she was known as a prophetess in the land. King Josiah essentially told his leaders, "Talk to Huldah and see if God is going to rain down terror on us because of what our fathers have done and because of what we have allowed in the land. If I am king, then I am responsible."

Huldah gave the king's messengers a two-part response. In the first part of her message, she said God was going to do exactly what He had promised to do to Judah in the Book of the Law because the people had worshiped false gods. In the second part, the prophetess said God was pleased with King Josiah:

> Tell the king of Judah, who sent you to inquire of the LORD, "This is what the LORD, the God of Israel, says concerning the words you heard: Because *your heart was responsive* and *you humbled yourself* before the LORD when you heard what I have spoken against this place and its people, that they would become accursed and laid waste, and because *you tore your robes* and *wept in my presence*, I have heard you, declares the LORD." (2 Kings 22:18–19, italics mine)

From that day forward King Josiah went on a campaign to clean up Judah. He was still only twenty-six, but he was not worried about being politically correct. He helped his men tear down idols, destroy unholy shrines and places of worship, dig up the bones of wicked priests and leaders, and arrest all of the wizards and soothsayers in Judah. This man was possessed with a cause.

FOUR CHARACTERISTICS OF PEOPLE WHO FIND THEIR DESTINY

King Josiah exhibited four key characteristics found in the lives of people who have found their destiny in God. If you want to become the Ultimate Champion, you need to find out what God wants you to do with your life—then do it! Do you have these characteristics in your heart and life?

1. *They have a tender heart.*

Huldah the prophetess essentially told King Josiah, "God told me to speak to you in a different manner because your heart was tender." You know you have a tender heart if the things that bother God also bother you, and you feel the pain of people around you.

I saw this characteristic in action the day I went to lunch with Lee Haney in Atlanta. Lee is an eight-time Mr. Olympia bodybuilding champion, a born-again Christian, and a popular speaker. We were about to enter a restaurant when a man suddenly ran up to Lee. He wore a backpack and carried some trinkets he was trying to sell. I thought, *Oh no, he's going to bug Lee.*

Haney started talking to the man. The next thing I knew, this guy walked into the cafeteria with us! Bothered by the fact that this man was hungry, Lee wanted to feed him. He didn't say, "Hey, John, I'm going to buy lunch for this guy." He simply and quietly took care of the man's need. It was natural for him to feel that man's pain and do something about it.

2. *They humble themselves before God.*

According to the Bible, Josiah not only had a tender heart, but he also humbled himself before God. I am always amazed by the fact that God uses "mess-ups." He has used adulterers, murderers, thieves, prostitutes, and political terrorists for His purposes. But there is one type of person God has not used—a proud person.

People who find their destiny have a tender heart and are humble before God. They know that without God they are finished. When someone pays you a compliment, you should tremble, not gloat. The moment you take a compliment into your heart and truly believe it belongs to you, then you are in for big trouble. Why? We know from God's Word that He cannot and will not use a proud person.

3. They are moved with passion.

Has your passion for God outweighed your fear of failure? God noticed when Josiah was so moved by His Word and by his nation's failure to honor it that he tore his clothes and wept. Josiah's passion for God outweighed his fear. He also didn't want to miss the responsibility and the purpose for which he had been born.

Josiah became king when he was only eight, so he was being served the equivalent of "cookies and milk" on gold platters when the crown was first placed on his head. That means that up until the day he heard the Book of the Law read out loud, Josiah was probably just a mild-mannered king. Then he discovered that the heart of God grieved because of his nation.

Are you passionate about the reason and purpose for your birth? Do you understand why God put you on this earth? When you are passionate about the same things God is passionate about, then you will find your destiny. God created you that way. You will never find your destiny until the things that move God also move you.

Some people can sit through any sermon and witness any miracle, yet still focus their thoughts on where they are going to have lunch! Nothing seems to move or shake them. You are in a dangerous position when you have no passion for the things of God.

We must fan the flames of our passion for God's purpose in our lives and *get on with the job*. I am possessed with this sense that we—the people of God—have to *do something*. I believe Josiah was blessed because was committed to being a do-something king.

4. They wake up in the middle of their destiny.

We are so close to the second coming of Christ that you should have no doubt that God made you for such a time as this. When you follow your passion for God, you will wake up right in the middle of your destiny. Honestly, that is all that matters in our brief span of life on this planet. You will also begin to experience the blessings of God's favor upon your life.

King Josiah came face to face with his destiny when he began to obey God's commands by tearing down idols and evil worship sites. Everything seemed to become clear on that day Josiah saw a particular tombstone on a mountainside in Bethel:

> The king asked, "What is that tombstone I see?" The men of the city said, "It marks the tomb of the man of God who came from Judah and pronounced against the altar of Bethel the very things you have done to it." (2 Kings 23:17).

The people in that area knew the history of the man buried in that tomb. They essentially told Josiah, "This guy prophesied that you would be standing here doing exactly what you're doing!" In that moment, King Josiah realized he had been born for that moment in time. He stood right in the middle of destiny.

EVERY DAY BURSTS WITH THE URGENCY OF DESTINY

You and I are in the same situation. We are living in a crucial period in human history when every day seems to burst with the urgency of destiny. I sense that mankind is poised at the brink of "the fullness of time."

God brought each of us here for a specific purpose and plan. We can't afford to simply go through the motions of the Christian life concentrating on what we can get. God put us here to make a difference; that is His priority for our lives.

King Josiah was a man who discovered and fulfilled his destiny in God. Listen to what the Bible says about him:

> Neither before nor after Josiah was there a king like him
> *who turned to the LORD as he did—with all his heart* and
> with all his soul and with all his strength, in accordance
> with all the Law of Moses (2 Kings 23:25, italics mine).

That is powerful! *Josiah became passionate about his destiny.* He went from being a nice king who did a good job, to a leader who tore his clothes in passionate repentance for his nation. By his actions he declared, "God made me for this!"

We need to get past just being nice, quiet Christians. We need to be moved emotionally and passionately. God had a reason for putting us here in this time and season. You have a divine purpose and destiny to make a difference for Him!

Larry Jones, the founder of Feed the Children, has made a great impact on my life and on the lives of millions of hungry people around the world. Did you know that he discovered his destiny by doing what Jesus would do for *one person*?

WOULD YOU INVEST TWENTY CENTS IN YOUR DESTINY?

In 1979 Larry Jones was a traveling evangelist when he visited Port Au Prince, Haiti, and was approached by a little nine-year-old boy. The boy said, "Lorri (mispronouncing Larry's name), would you give me a nickel for a roll?"

Larry said, "Sure, I'll give you a nickel."

The boy added, "Lorri, could you give me three more cents? If you give me three more cents, they will cut the roll in half and put butter on both sides."

Larry said, "Sure. Get some butter on both sides. Now you need something to wash it down, don't you? How much is a Coke?"

When the boy said, "Twelve cents," Larry Jones gave the lad a total of twenty cents and watched him walk away with a smile on his face. That little encounter so affected Larry that when he returned to the United States, he read the Bible from cover to cover, searching for every reference about feeding the poor and taking care of the hungry. Then he did a television program and mentioned what happened to him with the little boy in Haiti. He also mentioned that the United States had 35 million metric tons of wheat stored in grain elevators. Larry said, "If we could just get a piece of bread to the hungry, it will open their hearts to the gospel."

Within a few weeks after the program aired, fifty truckloads of wheat were donated to Larry's ministry! Thus began Feed the Children. This year that organization will supply more than $250 million worth of food and other supplies to needy children around the world. Remember where it all began—with a simple gift of *twenty cents* to a hungry nine-year-old boy in Haiti.

JESUS OFTEN COMES IN DISGUSTING DISGUISES

Is your heart easily moved? Remember that this is one of the four characteristics of people who have discovered the reason they were born. I talked to Larry Jones about compassion and helping the poor. He told me, "Mother Teresa said, 'Jesus comes to us in disgusting disguises.'" This humble nun won the world's respect through her faithful service to India's poor. She knew what she talked about because she poured out her life to help people who could never offer her anything in return. Mother Teresa found her destiny and spent her life fulfilling God's call to the needy, the sick, and the outcasts. Many times she discovered she did God's perfect will when she accepted the smelly, disgusting jobs that no one else wanted, such as caring for people who were dying from terrible diseases.

The unkempt drifter who came up to my friend Lee Haney in Atlanta appeared disgusting. I was turned off because he looked dirty and messy, and I really didn't like the fact that he sold trinkets. I learned an important lesson that day: Never judge anyone by his or her outward appearance. We all need to remember that Jesus said, "Assuredly, I say to you, inasmuch as you did it to one of the least of these My brethren, you did it to Me" (Matt. 25:40 NKJV). Larry Jones believes that is how Jesus comes to us—disguised as the "least" of us.

THERE'S MORE TO THE CHRISTIAN LIFE THAN SHOWING UP FOR CHURCH

You need to have a tender and humble heart before God, but you also need to be passionate about your role in God's purpose and plan for this generation and the next. You and I were born for such a time as this. If you really believe that God put you here with a plan and a purpose, then you know there is more to the Christian life than just showing up for a Sunday morning church service.

I once heard Billy Graham say that 70 percent of the people in church on Sunday morning don't really know Jesus. If you really know the Master, then you should also know that God created you with a divine purpose. The only way to discover that purpose in life is to turn to the Lord with your whole heart everyday. No, you don't have to "get saved again," but you need to do what Jesus expects all of us to do: "If anyone would come after me, he must deny himself and take up his cross *daily* and follow me" (Luke 9:23, italics mine).

If you aren't sure that God created you with a divine purpose, then I'll mention just a few things to help you. You may be a good person who would be quick to help somebody in need, and you may believe in God, but don't confuse religion with really knowing Jesus. Believing in God doesn't make you a Christian, and shedding a tear in a prayer to Jesus really doesn't make you a Christian either. You become a Christian when you surrender your life to Jesus. I also believe that this is the day you become ordained to be a *world shaker* and a *history maker* in your generation.

If you aren't sure about where you stand with Jesus Christ, then I urge you not to let one more minute go by not knowing what God has for you. I don't want you to feel condemned; I want you to ask God to forgive you so He can pick you up, patch you up, clean you up, and restore to you everything He has for you.

Will you surrender to Him?

This could be your day of destiny. Totally yield your life to the Lord Jesus and give everything to Him. If you are already sure you have given your heart to Jesus Christ, then your eternal destination is taken care of. Now you can concentrate on God's purpose for your life.

Begin by turning to God with your whole heart everyday. Study His Word as Josiah did to learn what He says about right and wrong. Commit yourself to doing what He says. Seek Him in prayer and praise and worship each day. This is the best way to discover and fulfill your destiny in life—and to become the Ultimate Champion. Nothing is more exciting than living a life that is totally sold out to the Lord. He wants to flood your life with His favor and blessing. These floodgates open when you turn to Him with your whole heart. It really doesn't get any better than this!

OVERCOME YOUR FAITH-STRIPPING GOLIATH

During the early days of the Power Team, I conducted a crusade in St. Louis, Missouri, with two other members of the team. One of the local couples helping with the crusade invited us to their apartment for spaghetti one night. They told us up front that they had a special reason for inviting us to their home—they wanted us to witness to the rough kids in their neighborhood who daily gathered in front of their apartment complex.

We gladly accepted their invitation. Sure enough, when we entered the apartment complex, we saw a group of rough-looking teenagers sitting outside the apartment building. After dinner, our hosts said, "Will you go outside with us and try to witness to these neighborhood kids?"

On the way out the door, I thought, *I have a steel bar, a hot-water bottle, and a pair of handcuffs in the car. If we're going to witness to these kids, then I'm going to tell them to get all of their friends, and we'll do a miniature Power show!*

We talked to about twenty teens at 8:30 that night and told them what we planned to do. Within an hour there were fifty of the roughest kids I'd ever seen waiting for us. I blew up the hot-water bottle, bent the steel bar with my teeth, and snapped the handcuffs while the group watched closely. Then I began to preach to them. I sensed the presence and the anointing of God begin to come upon us as I asked the teenagers, "Now, who wants to accept the Lord?"

A WITCH'S SHRILL VOICE PIERCED THE DARKNESS

From behind me came the most piercing, blood-curdling scream I have ever heard, followed by the shrill voice of a witch that pierced the darkness with the taunting words: "Don't believe him. There is no God!"

Immediately I sensed the presence of the most demonic force I had ever encountered. Instinctively, I turned around to find the source of this demonic power, and I saw a woman dressed in black from head to toe walking out of an empty field beside the apartment complex. I can still see the woman's long black hair flowing in the wind. It appeared as if her feet weren't even touching the ground when she walked.

Before I knew it, she was upon us. I stood face to face with a full-blown witch! Her voice was so piercing, shrill, and antagonistic that she successfully diverted every one of those young people from committing their lives to Christ. I knew I was locked into a direct, face-to-face showdown with evil, but the Lord had given me such a supernatural boldness that I knew I wouldn't fail.

God will also give you this same boldness every time you take a stand for Him—no matter who or what tries to impede you. Remember that confrontations with evil aren't won by human might or power but by the Spirit of God at work through you.

Don't back down. Just step up to the battle line and stand your ground.

I spoke to the witch, and she began to openly challenge me in front of the teenagers. They didn't know it, but the battle was over *their souls*, and eternal destinies were on the line. In that moment the Lord gave me an idea. "You are pretty daring to walk up here and talk like this," I said. She was pleased at my statement. She didn't know, however, that God had shown me how to lay a trap for her, using her own pride for bait.

"You would probably take any dare I'd give you just to prove you're right," I continued. "In fact, you probably have the guts to say *anything* I challenge you to say."

She said, "That's right. I'll say any cuss word you can imagine. That's my specialty."

I knew that God's trap was laid. I replied, "I know one thing you can't say."

IF NOTHING HAPPENS, THEN EVERYTHING I'VE SAID IS A LIE!

I challenged her right in front of those kids to say just one statement. I said, "If you say this statement and nothing happens to you, then everything I've said is a lie, and you are right—there is no God. But if you say this statement and something does happen to you, then you—and everyone else—will know there is a God in heaven."

She quickly answered my challenge. "I'll say it. I'll say anything!"

Every one of the teenagers leaned forward in awe as they watched the spiritual contest unfold.

The moment of truth had arrived. I looked that witch in the eye and said, "Say 'Jesus is Lord' three times, and then say 'I love You, Jesus' three times."

The witch suddenly recoiled and said, "Oh, I can't say *that.*"

So I answered just as quickly, "See?"

My answer seemed to prick her pride and nudge her beyond her fears. "I love Jesus, I love Jesus," she mocked. After only the second time she said those words, her voice suddenly cracked. Her body started shaking, and she began to cry uncontrollably. While fifty teenagers watched in amazement, this young witch dressed in black collapsed to the ground and crumpled up into a ball. She continued to weep and cry out in brokenness, repeating the words over and over again, "I love You, Jesus. I love You, Jesus. I love You, Jesus."

The Lord had shown me that if I could get this woman to publicly confess those words with her mouth, then He would break Satan's hold over her life and set her free. While she continued to weep like a little child, I led every one of those hardened teenagers to Jesus. I will never forget the scene after I'd prayed the "sinner's prayer" with those kids. As I walked away, that young lady—the former witch and servant of Satan—was still crumpled up in a little ball on the grass, crying sweetly like a little girl and repeating the words "I love You, Jesus."

I knew she meant what she said, and I also knew Jesus heard every word His long-lost daughter was saying to Him.

Are you ready to stretch your faith and dare to do something for God? There is something deep inside you that shouts, "Yes!" Yet it is only fair to give you this warning: Anytime you set out to do something for God, you are almost guaranteed to run into a few giants along the way. Don't be surprised if obstacles or problems come along that threaten to strip away your confidence and hope in God. When they do, you can turn those obstacles into stepping-stones to victory by letting God fight the battle. The Lord is ready and able to help you defeat your "giants" with the same spiritual weapons David used against Goliath many centuries ago.

GIANTS SHOUT THREATS
FROM THE VALLEY OF DESPAIR

We all face giant-sized problems in our nation today. There are giants standing in the valley of despair shouting threats at our families, our churches, and our nation. This is happening on a scale we haven't seen before. Americans weathered two World Wars and sent young soldiers to several unpopular military conflicts that nearly split the nation. Yet in our day, we reap the harvest of a conflict that has taken an even higher toll on us: the revolution of rebellion that swept across the country in the 1960s. It unleashed a flood of selfishness that has seriously disintegrated the foundation of our families a generation later.

The giants of the past were serious, but the giants we face today—rebellion, rampant drug use, sexual promiscuity, materialism, and extreme youth violence—are even worse, in a way, because they threaten not just adults, but our children. They attack us in our homes, schools, and neighborhoods instead of some country overseas.

Problems that used to taunt twenty-year-olds on college campuses are now threatening eleven-year-olds in elementary schools and at home. How do I know this? All I have to do is read the mail that floods into our ministry offices day after day. Some of the letters kids send us from around the country would shock you! I hear from children afraid they have AIDS and from young girls who speak of physical and sexual abuse and satanic rituals. They cry out for a Savior, and it is our task to give them the good news. They look for a modern-day David who has the courage to take a stand for a real God.

We live in a society where an average of about one million children a year are sexually abused or neglected,[34] and 4.4 million youths between the ages of twelve and twenty admit to "binge drinking" or heavy consumption of alcohol.[5] A wave of violence sweeps the country as parents kill their kids, kids kill their parents, and kids kill other kids. The Centers for Disease Control and Prevention says homicide—murder—is the second leading cause of death of persons fifteen to thirty-four years of age, and it has been the leading cause of death for African-Americans in this age group for more than a decade![6]

A recent poll conducted by NBC News and the *Wall Street Journal* found that "Americans are frightened by violent crimes committed by young people and worried that society's standards of behavior have eroded."[7] Three out of every four Americans told the pollsters they don't trust politicians when they talk about social and moral values. Of the people surveyed, 83 percent agreed that "parents not paying enough attention to what's going on in their children's lives" has become a "very serious problem."[8]

Everyone seems to be concerned about the influence of sexually explicit or violent media on our children, the high rate of divorce, and the breakup of the families in America. At the same time, only 4 percent of the people questioned "thought the federal government had the most potential to repair America's moral fabric."[9] It seems as if America and its self-help armies are lined up in fear, while the giants taunt us from the valley of failure.

GIANT-SIZED PROBLEMS
PRESENT GIANT-SIZED OPPORTUNITIES!

I believe you and I are living in a season of giants—a season marked by giant-sized problems and giant-sized opportunities to stand up for Jesus Christ. The Bible refers to another person who lived in a season of giants. His name was David, and the first giant he faced was Goliath. Goliath's name in Hebrew essentially means "to strip and captivate."[10]

Then Goliath, a Philistine champion from Gath, came out of the Philistine ranks to face the forces of Israel. He was a giant of a man, measuring over nine feet tall! He wore a bronze helmet, a two-hundred-pound coat of mail, bronze leggings, and carried a bronze javelin several inches thick, tipped with a twenty-five-pound iron spearhead, and his armor bearer walked ahead of him with a huge shield. (1 Sam. 17:4–7 TLB)

Goliath measured approximately nine feet, nine inches tall, and somehow I think he was one ugly giant! If you look closely at what this giant shouted at the Israelite soldiers, you can also tell that he was very shrewd. He had a specific strategy in mind when he stood up in the valley to challenge the army of Israel:

He [Goliath] stood and shouted across to the Israelis, "Do you need a whole army to settle this? I will represent the Philistines, and you choose someone to represent you, and we will settle this in single combat! If your man is able to kill me, then we will be your slaves. But if I kill him, then you must be our slaves! I defy the armies of Israel! Send me a man who will fight with me!" (1 Sam. 17:8–10 TLB)

Goliath Wanted to Strip and Captivate God's People

The soldiers of Israel shook in their sandals when Goliath screamed out, "I defy the armies of Israel." They really began to quiver when the giant narrowed it down to, "Send *one man* who will fight with me!" That was no accident. Goliath didn't want the Israelites to realize their power as a unified army, so his tactic was to isolate and intimidate them one on one. Above all, he wanted the army of Israel to forget who they were—the children of God.

Goliath wanted to strip God's people of their faith so he could take captive their destiny. He almost succeeded—until a certain teenager walked on the scene.

There were probably ten thousand other young men who were just as strong and talented as David, and most of them probably believed that God *could* use them. David, on the other hand, believed God *would* use him. He was the only one who dared face the giant who was holding everybody else in the bondage of fear.

A lot of people sit in church every weekend thinking that God *could* use them. It is time for us to stand up for a cause and say, "God *will* use me to make a difference in my nation, in my city, and in my area!"

Your first obstacle may come in the form of opposition by relatives or close friends who disapprove of your zeal for God. You might have to do what David did when he told his angry brother, "What have I now done? *Is there not a cause?* And he turned from him toward another . . ." (1 Sam. 17:29–30 KJV, italics mine).

Even King Saul questioned David's faith and methods, but David held his ground and told the king: "The LORD who delivered me from the paw of the lion and the paw of the bear, He will deliver me from the hand of this Philistine." And Saul said to David, "Go, and the LORD be with you" (1 Sam. 17:37 NKJV).

The Bible tells us David reached down and picked up five smooth stones before he went out to face Goliath. I don't think he picked up the extra stones because he thought he might miss. David really believed there was no way he could lose. He picked up five smooth stones because he knew that Goliath belonged to a *family* of giants. He had four brothers in the Philistine army who were almost as big as he was.

When you live in a land of giants, you always need to plan for more than just one confrontation. David picked up *five* smooth stones just in case those brothers didn't run for the hills that day. He was ready to load up his slingshot and start after them, too, if necessary. You also need to be ready.

Intimidation Ran in Goliath's Family

I've known about Goliath's brothers for many years, but I never heard anyone say much about them. When I began to search the Scriptures for information about these giants, I discovered that intimidation ran in Goliath's family. It runs in Satan's spiritual family too. He sends giants to block our path and to bluff us out of what God has for our lives. These giants want to intimidate us so we will surrender to fear and insecurity, then abandon our faith in God's ability to win the battle.

David stood out from the faithless crowd, but he was only doing what every believer who knows Jesus Christ should do. He essentially told King Saul, "Look, I've been in some fights before this. I wasn't afraid then, and I'm not afraid now. My God delivered me then, and He'll deliver me now."

We need to remember the victories as David did. We need to keep telling our families, our children, and our friends about all the miracles God has performed in our lives. I am convinced that many of the young people raised in Christian homes turn away from God and adopt ungodly lifestyles because parents quit telling the stories of His miracles and provision. We need to tell our children the stories of "the lion and the bear" so that when they face their Goliath, they'll say, "Wait a minute—the same God who saved my mother, the same God who saved my father, will save me too!"

David spoke his final words to the giant who stood in front of him, and then he ran to meet him in battle:

> David said to the Philistine, "You come against me with sword
> and spear and javelin, but I come against you in the name of the
> LORD Almighty, the God of the armies of Israel, whom you have

dcficd. This day the LORD will hand you over to me, and I'll strike you down and cut off your head. Today I will give the carcasses of the Philistine army to the birds of the air and the beasts of the earth, and the whole world will know that there is a God in Israel. All those gathered here will know that it is not by sword or spear that the LORD saves; for the battle is the LORD's, and he will give all of you into our hands." (1 Sam. 17:45–47)

David was not going to allow this giant to strip God's people of their destiny. We need to have the same mentality today. It is time for you and me to take our stand and say, "Is there not a cause? The devil is not going to strip my kids, my friends, or my family of their destiny!"

David's life reveals the third key principle for becoming the Ultimate Champion:

> *Overcome the "giants" who want to strip away your faith*
> *by knowing your God. Then you will know you cannot*
> *lose.*

POTS BEGAN TO SHAKE,
AND DOGS BEGAN TO HOWL!

While I was attending Bible college in Florida, the Lord taught me some vital lessons about spiritual warfare that I will never forget. I was still ministering through small-scale Power Team crusades, and I also helped out with the youth at a local church. A mother of one of the young ladies in our youth group called the church and said, "My daughter is acting strange. I think she's showing demonic manifestations. Can somebody come over and pray for her?"

Someone at the church asked me to follow up on the call since

I was a Bible school student and helping with the youth. I didn't know what to expect when I went up to this family's house, so I was relieved when a sweet, motherly lady opened the door. As soon as I stepped into the house, the woman's fourteen-year-old daughter walked into the room. She looked as if she was twenty years old. She was very attractive but overly made-up.

When I talked to her, she seemed very pleasant. I didn't see anything strange going on until I began to pray for her. Suddenly her grip on my wrist began to get very strong, and her face began to turn colors, changing from blue to red to green! Then the pots on the kitchen walls began to shake, and all of the dogs in the neighborhood began howling and scratching at the back door of the house. The phone started ringing, and when I picked it up, no one was on the line. In fact, the phone just kept on ringing, no matter how often we answered it.

Suddenly the girl began to speak in some kind of demonic language that I felt clearly was linked to witchcraft in some way. I was so startled, scared, and overwhelmed by it all that I ended the prayer and left.

The girl's mother called the next day and said her daughter had admitted that she worshiped Satan and that she had been seeing a witch. Then she tore up the house. She begged me, "Would you please come back?" We found out later that she had also been sleeping with older men as a result of her involvement in witchcraft and the occult.

I wasn't really excited about the thought of returning to that place, but I had been studying the power of praise, and the Holy Spirit brought to my mind Psalm 149:

> May the praise of God be in their mouths
>   and a double-edged sword in their hands,
> to inflict vengeance on the nations

and punishment on the peoples,
to bind their kings with fetters,
    their nobles with shackles of iron,
to carry out the sentence written against them.
    This is the glory of all his saints.
Praise the LORD. (Ps. 149:6–9)

We actually exercise judgment upon the devil and place hand-cuffs on his chief demons when we praise the name of the Lord. None of it happens through our own strength, ability, or fighting power. When I returned to the house, the same nice mother met me at the door, but this time the girl had an evil smile on her face from the moment I arrived. As soon as I began to pray for this young lady again, she began to mutter like a witch. This time I sensed the Lord tell me, "Quit trying to cast out this thing. Quit trying to pray about it. Just pronounce judgment upon the demonic forces and declare that their time is up."

I SPOKE DIRECTLY TO THE EVIL SPIRITS

I looked right into the girl's eyes. It was obvious that demons were operating through her. She began to levitate, and her face began to change colors again. I sensed that the demonic presence in the room was incredibly strong, but this time I wasn't as surprised or frightened. I spoke directly to the evil spirits manipulating this girl, saying: "In the name of Jesus, I pronounce judgment upon you, demons. Your time is up with this young lady, and I claim her salvation from this day forward. I pronounce her free in the name of the Lord Jesus Christ!" Then I turned around and walked out.

I didn't see any dramatic changes that day, but I knew I had obeyed God by authoritatively pronouncing judgment and sentencing the demonic forces in the name of Jesus Christ. Two days later, when she walked through her house and passed through a room where her mother was listening to a radio preacher, this girl suddenly fell flat on her face. When she stood up, she was weeping and worshiping God with her hands raised.

I didn't see her again until three years later when she came up to me at Lakeland First Assembly of God in Florida. She shared her full testimony with me. There was a glow all around her! I have never seen someone's face shine like that as she told me the Lord had set her free.

The Lord wants to teach us all how to conduct spiritual warfare His way—by taking authority over the enemy with God's high praises in our mouths. Then we can execute the judgment written in God's Word. Jesus said, "Whatever you bind on earth will be bound in heaven, and whatever you loose on earth will be loosed in heaven" (Matt. 16:19).

God is still empowering His people to take away the enemy's weapons of destruction, just as David claimed Goliath's deadly sword after God won the battle. I will never forget the letter we received from a fourteen-year-old girl in Wisconsin, who wrote:

Dear John Jacobs and the Power Team,

I saw you on June 9th at the Believer's Church in Marshfield, and I want to thank you for saving my life. That night when I got home I was going to slit my wrist. If it hadn't have been for you, I would be dead right now. I love you guys. Thank you so much.
Here is the blade that I was going to use to slit my wrist . . .

We found a doubled-edged razor blade carefully packed in the envelope with the letter. We knew we were looking at yet another weapon of destruction that God had confiscated from the devil. Honestly, we *can* take authority over the devil and end his illegal reign over America's young people, but we need to run to the battle with boldness as children of God. Run to meet your Goliath with God's praises on your lips, and remember to claim the enemy's weapons of destruction as trophies of his defeat by God's power.

DEFEAT THE GIANT OF DISCOURAGEMENT

Discouragement is one of the most common obstacles we face in this life. It is also one of Satan's most effective tools for defeating unprepared Christians. One of the most discouraging—and dramatic—challenges I have ever faced occurred in South Africa more than twelve years ago. The Power Team conducted a crusade in a suburb of Johannesburg, the nation's capital city. We held the meetings in an auditorium that was designed to seat about eight thousand people safely—but every night of the crusade from ten to twelve thousand people squeezed into the building.

In fact, the way the people were lined up in the place made it a firetrap just waiting for a spark to trigger a catastrophe. There were so many people in the auditorium that we couldn't see any exits or aisles. From our viewpoint on the stage, the size of the crowd was overwhelming.

Just before we began the crusade meeting on the first night, the sponsoring pastor came up to me and said, "Have you prayed *extra*?

Did you know this auditorium is located next to one of the satanic headquarters of the world?"

I said, "No, to be honest with you, I haven't prayed any more than usual."

He looked at me and said, "Well, maybe you should."

It just so happened that I had prepared a message for that night that labeled the devil as a five-time loser. I planned to take the audience through the Bible, highlighting key Scripture passages that describe how Satan lost the power of God through rebellion, then demonstrating his failures from beginning to end. My main point: If you aren't serving God, then you are serving a five-time loser. If you are serving evil, then you have hooked up with the biggest loser in the history of the universe. The devil just wants to take you down with him.

I began to preach the message that night and told the crowd that the devil isn't what the world portrays him to be—a slick leader rich in sensuality and power. The truth is that he is a five-time loser, a counterfeit operating under the camouflage of a lion skin—but having no teeth. Things were going well until I said, "Point number one."

I gave the Scripture reference. Suddenly every light in the auditorium went out. Even the sound system went dead because the electricity had been cut off.

I'LL MAKE THE PEOPLE PANIC, AND HUNDREDS WILL BE KILLED!

I couldn't see anything. Even the emergency lights went out! In that moment, I could sense the devil tell me, "I am going to make these people panic, and hundreds are going to be killed. You had better announce that *this meeting is over* and tell everybody to file out."

I was discouraged, and everything in me wanted to give in to this fear, but I mustered up all the faith I could find. Stepping up to the edge of the platform and raising both of my hands, I screamed out as loud as I could, "In the name of Jesus, I rebuke you, devil! You cannot stop this meeting, and in the name of the Lord Jesus Christ I command these lights to come back on!" Instantly the lights came back on. The crowd was amazed.

Now the critics might say, "It was just coincidence." However, this happened exactly the same way *every single time* I made another point describing the devil as a five-time loser! I continued preaching without incident until I said, "Point number two." Once again, the power went out as I read the Scripture. The auditorium was plunged into total darkness. And once again, I heard the same discouraging words whispered to my spirit. I had to step up to the edge of the platform and shout out the same rebuke and command in the name of Jesus to get the power turned back on so I could continue. This happened five times in one night.

By the time I reached the point where I planned to give an altar call, the people were sitting on the edge of their seats with their fingers clenched. They had never seen such an open manifestation of spiritual warfare like they saw that night. When I made the altar call, I used the enemy's tactics against him by saying, "If this doesn't prove to you that there is a God in heaven, and there is also a devil fighting against us in this meeting, then I don't know what else I can say." More than two thousand people immediately stood to their feet to receive Jesus Christ as Lord and Savior.

I sensed that God wasn't finished that night. I stepped forward to the platform and breathed a silent prayer, "Lord Jesus, what is going on here?" The Holy Spirit said to my heart, "One of the devil's leaders is here. Call him out. I want to save even him. But the devil is telling him that he is going to be killed tonight. Tell him the God that can save him can also protect his life."

I moved forward to the edge of the platform and said, "There is a satanic leader here, and the Lord says to you, 'Thus saith the Lord, that the same God who can save you can also protect you if you will come to Him now.'" Then I gave the command, "Stand up and come up here."

Suddenly a man seated in the back of the auditorium stood up, stepped to the crowded aisle and began to walk forward—and between thirty to forty people began to follow him! Honestly, I wasn't prepared for what I saw in that moment. Two of the people following him were women who fell to the ground and began to worm their way down the aisle like two snakes with their hands to their sides and their feet together. It looked as if two human beings had become snakes.

CLUMPS OF DIRT HUNG FROM THE MAN'S BODY

One of the men following the leader looked as if he lived in a graveyard. All of the Power Team members later confirmed that they saw actual clumps of dirt hanging from this man's body, attached by roots of some kind. As strange as these characters were, the man they followed was even worse, even though he was a well-dressed man. As he marched down the aisle with his followers and stood right in front of me, I was shocked when I noticed that his eyes were completely black. There was no white in his eyes. It looked as if he only had two big black pupils!

I didn't know what to do as all these weird people stood right in front of me. Surrounded by people who were obviously possessed by demons, the satanic leader just stood there. One woman was constantly grinding her teeth so loudly that I could hear it where I stood. Some of the other people barked like dogs, and then there was the man standing there with clumps of dirt hanging from his body.

All I knew to do was to raise both of my hands and cry out as loud as I could, "Jesus! Jesus!" Suddenly a strong wind blew through the auditorium like a tornado, and all of us heard and felt it. Then every one of the people in front of me—the satanic leader and all of his followers—suddenly collapsed to the floor because of the power of God's presence. When they finally began to stand up one by one, they rose with their hands in the air, praising and worshiping God.

THE SPIRIT OF THE LORD IS HERE TO FREE YOU FROM WITCHCRAFT!

When the satanic leader finally stood to his feet, he also raised his hands and began to praise and worship God. This time when I looked in his eyes, they had clearly changed from being totally black to a normal appearance. Best of all, the expression of his face had changed. In that moment I said to the audience, "The Spirit of the Lord is here to free you from witchcraft, the occult, astrology, black magic, and voodoo!" Hundreds of people began to run to the front of the auditorium. Many were set free even before they reached the front.

That was the day the Lord showed me that we should never be afraid to shout back at the devil. That was also the day I learned how to overcome discouragement. Since then, I've learned that discouragement is one of the giants the enemy sends our way anytime we say yes to God. Discouragement is one of the obstacles linked to Goliath and his four brothers.

Goliath came from a long line of giants, and intimidation ran in Goliath's family. The spirits that operated through this family were, and still are, ruled by Satan, the master intimidator. Goliath's first brother was named Ishbi-Benob. The meaning for this Hebrew name is "discouragement." Believe me, this giant lived up to his name. Ishbi-Benob escaped the first showdown with David, but he showed up again in the book of Second Samuel:

> Once again there was a battle between the Philistines and Israel. David went down with his men to fight against the Philistines, and he became exhausted. And Ishbi-Benob, one of the descendants of Rapha [the giant], whose bronze spearhead weighed three hundred shekels and who was armed with a new sword, said he would kill David. But Abishai son of Zeruiah came to David's rescue; he struck the Philistine down and killed him. (2 Sam. 21:15–17)

THE GIANT OF DISCOURAGEMENT HAS A BIG EGO AND A SHORT MEMORY

This overconfident giant was carrying a new sword, and he publicly announced that he was going to kill David. Do you know why he was carrying a new sword? David took the family sword from Goliath after he beheaded the giant with it. That was an insult to Goliath's family because his relatives had probably passed down that sword from family head to family head for many generations. For countless years, that family of wicked giants had probably bragged about all of the evil things they had done with that sword, but David made it into a trophy of defeat.

When Goliath's oldest brother, Ishbi-Benob, finally got the shiny new sword he had ordered, his ego seemed to take on new dimensions. The same giant who ran for his life the day young David killed his brother years before somehow felt as if he no longer had to fear David—or the God who fought for him. That was a big mistake.

The Bible tells us that David was exhausted when Ishbi-Benob showed up with his inflated ego and brand-new sword. The giant probably thought that victory was a sure thing since David was tired. But Ishbi-Benob had forgotten that he should truly be worried, not about David, but about David's God.

The apostle Paul tells us how to fight battles against evil in his letter to the Ephesian church:

> Finally, be strong in the Lord and in his mighty power. Put on the full armor of God so that you can take your stand against the devil's schemes. For our struggle is not against flesh and blood, but against the rulers, against the authorities, against the powers of this dark world and against the spiritual forces of evil in the heavenly realms. (Eph. 6:10–12)

I think David knew this truth when he ran to meet Goliath in battle armed only with a slingshot and five smooth stones. He knew the only way he could win was for God to fight the battle for him. Goliath and each of his four brothers were really only "tools" used by evil spirits. It was the custom in those days for a person's name to describe their nature, calling, or destiny. Goliath's brothers simply shouted whatever evil spirit operated through their lives.

THE SPIRIT OF DISCOURAGEMENT USES FEAR TO PLAY ON YOUR INSECURITIES

The evil spirit that operated through Goliath is still at work on the earth, and he still shouts at us, "I defy you! You are nothing!" His name means "to strip," so he does everything he can to strip God's people of their faith and courage. Ishbi-Benob's name means "discouragement," and the evil spirit that operated through his life screamed, "It's hopeless! You are going to fail. You will never make it."

The evil spirit of discouragement that inspired Ishbi-Benob is also still at work in the earth today, and it wants to bluff you out of what God has for you. He uses fear to play on your insecurities. He will constantly taunt you by saying, "Can't you feel the discouragement! Give it up! You are going to fail. There is no way you are going to make it."

I once read a statistic that as many as seventy million Americans suffer from depression at one time or another. The Power Team ministered in more than one hundred sixty churches in 1999 alone. To be honest, I have never seen so many discouraged Christians in my life! If you battle disappointment, I want to encourage you to remember the rest of the story:

> And Ishbi-Benob, one of the descendants of Rapha [the giant], whose bronze spearhead weighed three hundred shekels and who was armed with a new sword, said he would kill David. But Abishai son of Zeruiah came to David's rescue; he struck the Philistine down and killed him. (2 Sam. 21:16–17)

The original giant of discouragement was struck down by Abishai. *That's great. So what?* you may be thinking. Remember that in David's day, a man's name often described his destiny and calling in God. Abishai's name in the Hebrew means "the faithfulness of God." God wants us to tap the same cure for discouragement.

When David was too weak to defend himself against the giant of discouragement, was God worried? Absolutely not. The battle wasn't David's fight to begin with. It was God who defeated Goliath, and it was God who defeated the discouragement of Ishbi-Benob with the faithfulness of God in Abishai. This is incredibly important for you and me. There is absolutely no doubt that some day, in some way, you and I will come face to face with the giant of discouragement. We also know that when it happens,

53

this giant will shout in our faces, and to our families and friends, "It's hopeless! You are not going to make it. Give it up—you are going to fail."

In that moment, whether we feel weak or strong, foolish or wise, we need to remember that the battle is not ours. God will win our battle against discouragement the same way He won David's battle with this giant: *He will defeat discouragement with His own faithfulness.* This is the fourth key principle for becoming the Ultimate Champion.

Abishai was an interesting man in Bible history. He was one of David's most loyal men. David had a total of four hundred soldiers who were called "mighty men." Among this elite group were thirty superheroes, and the chief among them was Abishai, the "faithfulness of God."

The next time the devil tries to discourage you by sending the giant of discouragement to block your path or threaten your destiny with the taunting words, "You are not going to make it, you are going to fail," remember Abishai.

Tell the devil: "The Bible says the same God who called me will carry it on to completion. Any good work God starts, He will see through because My God is faithful. Sarah was able to give birth to a baby even though she was ninety years old because she knew that God was faithful, and He had promised she would have a baby" (Phil. 1:6; Heb. 11:11).

Do you realize that God doesn't know how to be unfaithful, even when we are unfaithful? It is part of His character to be faithful. So, when discouragement comes your way, say to yourself, "God has begun a good work in me, and He will see it through."

Several years ago a young lady sent an unforgettable letter to the Power Team in which she described God's faithfulness to deliver her from impossible circumstances:

Dear Mr. Jacobs and The Power Team:

Thank you for taking the time out of your busy schedule to visit my high school. It is a dream come true—to finally get to see you after all the years of inspiration that you have been to me.

A few years ago my life totally fell apart. My brother was raping me and abusing me every day. My parents basically disowned me. I was drinking heavily and using drugs every day. I also tried to kill myself almost every day. But worst of all, I was also pregnant with my brother's child, and was basically living off of the streets. I was ready to give up.

Then one day I was at my friend's house, and we started watching the Power Team. It was the first time I had ever watched TBN, and it was the first time I had ever heard anyone talk about Jesus Christ. I was amazed by how I could relate to every one of the [Power Team] members, the drug use, and the abuse in their past. However, I did not understand how Jesus could change someone's life so much.

I began to get curious about Jesus and started going to the library to read the Bible (because I did not own one). After about three weeks of watching the Power Team and learning about the Bible, and hearing all of the inspiring stories from the team, I went to church for the first time in my life.

Now I would not trade my life for anything else in the world. I have a beautiful daughter who is almost four. I am very active in school and am graduating from high school this year. I also have plans to go to college. I have stopped using drugs and alcohol and now am very active in a local church. I love my life now. Once again, thank you for taking the time to come to our school.

This young woman had been stripped of all hope for the future. She was a victim of the same spirit of discouragement that operated through Goliath's first brother, Ishbi-Benob. Yet, God carefully orchestrated the events in her life to expose her to His faithfulness in Jesus Christ. Though she was rejected by her parents and abused by her brother, this young woman mattered to God. He saved her soul and restored her hope for tomorrow. He put her feet on solid ground and gave her a future.

The next time you face the giant of discouragement, shout in the giant's face, "My God is faithful!" If you can't find anyone to encourage you, then encourage yourself with the Word of God by saying:

God doesn't love me based on my performance. God loves me because He can't help Himself. No matter how many times I've failed or how many mistakes I've made, Jesus paid for them all on the cross.

The Bible says in Psalm 3, "O LORD, how many are my foes! How many rise up against me! Many are saying of me, 'God will not deliver him.' But you are a shield around me, O LORD; you bestow glory on me and lift up my head." The Bible also says, "If God is for us, who can be against us?" (Ps. 3:2-3, Rom. 8:31b)

Whip the giant with the power of God's Spirit and say, "The battle is the Lord's because my God is faithful." Through the faithfulness of God, you will be able to tell the world the same thing this young woman told us in her letter: "Now I would not trade my life for anything else in the world."

TRUST GOD AND DESTROY THE DESTROYER

Don Fristch, a retired Army colonel and the executive director of crusades for the Power Team, decided one Friday morning to visit the booth the ministry had set up at a pastor's conference hosted by Bishop T.D. Jakes and The Potter's House in the Dallas/Fort Worth area. On that morning God would reveal a part of Don's past that very few people knew about. He also would demonstrate to two people just how far He would go to deliver His children from certain disaster.

Don had planned to spend only four hours at the booth that day before heading back to the Power Team office. Something happened, however, that transformed his day—and his life. An African-American pastor approached the booth. When Don greeted him, he noticed that the man wore a small Silver Star pin on his lapel—it was an exact duplicate, in miniature, of the Silver Star ribbon awarded by the armed forces for acts of valor.

After the men talked about the ministry of the Power Team, Don said, "I see that you served in the military." The African-American pastor nodded and said, "Yes, I served in the U. S. Army for about twenty-six years."

Don said, "I served in the Army, too, for about thirty-three years."

The pastor's eyes lit up. "Oh, then you must have spent some time in Vietnam."

"Yes, I served three tours in Vietnam," Don answered.

The pastor said he had served two tours there.

Things began to get interesting for Don. "Well, I was there very early on."

The pastor said, "So was I! I was there in the early 1960s."

"You might not know about this organization, but I was in one of the first attack helicopter units that the Army ever had. It was called the UTT, which stands for Utility Tactical Transport Helicopter Company. It was misnamed because we weren't carrying anything; we were gunships."

I FELT AS IF I WERE GOING TO MEET JESUS THAT DAY

"Well, let me tell you about that. I am *fully* aware of your organization," the pastor said. "During my first tour in Vietnam, I was an advisor to a Vietnamese army mechanized rifle company. We were caught in an ambush, and we came under a brutal fire from enemy forces. Many of the men in the column had already been killed, and the rest of us were being shredded by the intense gunfire of the larger Vietcong force. From the moment we came under attack, I began pleading with U.S. Military Headquarters in Saigon by two-way radio for some kind of military support or rescue operation. I really felt as if I was going to meet Jesus that day. But because of your unit, I am alive today."

Don said, "Well, that's amazing!"

The pastor added, "Yeah, what is more amazing is that I still remember the call sign of the individual from your unit who made first contact with me. His call sign was *Raider Two-Three*."

While Don listened for a few moments more, the pastor described just how impossible his rescue was. At that time there were only about five thousand Americans in Vietnam, and very few military bases existed. The only resources available to American military advisors in the field were those of the South Vietnamese army, plus the few American aircraft, which were mostly propeller-driven planes, and personnel based in the country at that time.

The complex communications network, coordinated air support, and well-supplied military strike forces wouldn't exist for at least four more years. All the radios in use at the time were "line-of-sight" units that wouldn't work if a mountain or some other obstruction blocked the signal path. As the senior American military advisor to this South Vietnamese unit, he knew from the beginning that his plea for help was probably useless—the trapped platoon would get out on their own, or they wouldn't get out at all. The latter was most likely.

In the middle of all the gunfire, the shouting, and the cries of the wounded, the lieutenant (pastor) suddenly heard his radio crackle as the impossible happened. An American voice crisply announced, "*This is Raider Two-Three. We're on our way!*"

The pastor continued, "Well, I've been doing all of the talking. Tell me a little bit about yourself. Tell me about your time in Vietnam."

Don said, "First, let me start the description of my Vietnam experience by introducing myself, brother. My name is *Raider Two-Three*."

The pastor nearly fell through the floor in shock. From that moment on, there was no more talk about Vietnam.

Both of the seasoned Vietnam veterans burst into tears. Their amazing story, spanning almost four decades, soon spread from the lobby to the pastors attending the conference. That pastor thought he was going to meet Jesus one day thirty-six years earlier, and instead, he made radio contact with an unsaved first lieutenant from New Rochelle, New York, leading a two-aircraft attack helicopter unit.

THE TWO ATTACK HELICOPTERS FIRED ROCKETS AT THE ENEMY

Don had received a vague launch order from an unknown source at Command Headquarters to help an American military advisor pinned down by the Vietcong. He was located southwest of Saigon near a map coordinate in an isolated patch of bamboo measuring one hundred yards square in the Delta Region. Don had never met the American advisor his unit saved that day, but he would never forget seeing the smoke rising from the fierce fire fight in the bamboo grove, and how he had to quickly decide where the enemy forces were located and where the "friendlies" were pinned down.

As soon as Don knew the situation on the ground, the two attack helicopters fired their rockets into the enemy locations and strafed the area with machine guns. Don also called for artillery and air support, which then consisted mostly of propeller-driven aircraft, and medical evacuation choppers known as MedEvac units.

The attack helicopters successfully broke the back of the Vietcong attack force, and the lieutenant and what remained of the Vietnamese unit were able to withdraw safely after the wounded had been picked up by MedEvac choppers. The battle was over within ninety minutes, but the emotions of the dramatic rescue lasted for a lifetime.

After the significance of their miraculous reunion had sunk in, the pastor told Don, "By the way, do you remember my call sign? It was *Migrant Two-Three.*"

"Of course, I remember Migrant Two-Three." That was Don's only link to the man whose life he'd saved, because he never landed his helicopter at the battle site. He stayed in the air and on guard while the medical units handled the duties on the ground.

Don completed two more tours in Vietnam, rising to the rank of colonel before he retired. Many years after the incident in the Delta, Don met Jesus Christ, and his life took a new path. Meanwhile, the lieutenant completed a second tour in Vietnam and ultimately became a pastor. Only God knew that thirty-six years later He would reunite these two men to show them how He had intervened in their lives for His own purposes.

GOD'S SUPERNATURAL INTERVENTION
ANNIHILATES THE DESTROYER

God intervened to save David from one of Goliath's brothers too. The second brother of Goliath shows up in the book of Second Samuel during yet another battle with David's mighty men: "In the course of time, there was another battle with the Philistines, at Gob. At that time Sibbecai the Hushathite killed Saph, one of the descendants of Rapha" (2 Sam. 21:18).

Saph's name means "destroyer" in the original Hebrew. The evil spirit that operated through Saph is still shouting at us today, "I'm going to *destroy* you. I am going to kill you and destroy your marriage. I will absolutely destroy the potential of God in you and wipe out your future."

God's modern answer to this blustering spiritual giant is the same answer He gave to Saph thousands of years ago. It is found in Sibbecai, the name of one of David's mighty men. Sibbecai was the soldier who killed Saph, and his name means "the supernatural intervention of God"!

With his threats and constant whispering, the devil may paint a picture for you that shows you going under. He wants you to believe that you are about to be destroyed, that you are finished. I want to show you the picture God has drawn for you in His unchanging Word. The good news is that God alone will determine the outcome of our lives once we say yes to Him. God's Word declares, "No eye has seen, no ear has heard, no mind has conceived what God has prepared for those who love him" (1 Cor. 2:9).

God has promised He will supernaturally intervene. Jesus Christ has already completed His work on the cross to "reverse the curse" and turn our lives around. The good news is that the supernatural intervention of God will kill the destroyer threatening your life every single time. If you feel that you are finished, if you are ready to give up and you feel like you are going under, call on His name. If the destroyer is threatening your marriage, your finances, your hope, or your joy, just stand and say, "My God will supernaturally intervene, for He is my sword and my shield; He is my glory and the lifter of my head!"

HAVE FAITH IN GOD AND LOOK FOR HIS SUPERNATURAL INTERVENTION

Don't be fooled. There is no doubt that someday, in some way, you and I will come face to face with a giant obstacle or problem that threatens to destroy us and everything dear to us. Our job is to *have faith in God and look for His supernatural intervention*. This is the fifth key principle for becoming the Ultimate Champion.

Yet, we have to remember that He is God, and we are not. It is His battle, and He will win it in the way, and in the time, that pleases Him. The most important thing for you to remember is that He is *for* you, and that settles the question of who comes out on top in the final analysis. Recall the Scripture that says, "You, dear children, are from God and have overcome them, because the one who is in you is greater than the one who is in the world" (1 John 4:4).

I have always believed in angels, but in recent years the Power Team has benefited from their protection many times. One time when the team was conducting crusades in the Denver area, my wife, Ruthanne, and a number of the team members' wives decided to go shopping using a rental car. The car was new, and it hardly had any miles on it, so they had no reason to worry about mechanical failure or car problems.

None of us realized that even as our wives drove away, television and radio stations throughout the city were broadcasting a breaking news story about a gunman with a high-powered machine gun who had just held up a bank and was shooting people. He had successfully eluded the police but was reportedly invading a number of homes and stopping cars in one specific location—the exact place where our wives were driving alone. They were totally unaware of the danger they faced.

THE GUNMAN IS EXTREMELY DANGEROUS AND ON THE LOOSE NEAR YOU

As the Power Team wives drove into the dangerous area where this gunman had been spotted, they noticed that there were police helicopters zooming overhead from time to time. When they turned on the radio, they heard all the stations warning drivers, "Stay in your cars! This heavily armed gunman is extremely dangerous, and he is on the loose in your area."

Suddenly, one of the tires on the new rental car blew out, so Ruthanne pulled the car over to the shoulder of the six-lane highway. They knew they were in a very dangerous situation, and they knew they couldn't get out to go for help. To their surprise, a young man seemed to appear out of nowhere and knocked on my wife's window. She knew better than to roll down her window, but she could clearly hear him say, "I want to fix your tire for you."

After a brief discussion with the other women in the car, Ruthanne carefully rolled down the driver's side window about two inches—just enough to give the trunk key to the young man. He quickly changed the tire and then returned the key to Ruthanne through the narrow opening in the window. Ruthanne wanted to reward this young Samaritan, so she glanced down for about two seconds to pull a twenty-dollar bill out of her wallet. When she looked up to hand the man the bill, she was shocked to find that he had vanished.

Ruthanne asked the other women in the car, "Did you see that?" They all began to search for any sign of the man, but no matter which way they looked, it was clear that he had vanished. The car was in a clear area where they could see in every direction for at least one hundred yards without obstruction. When all of the facts had been considered, all of the Power Team wives were convinced they had just been helped out of a potentially deadly situation by an angel. God had intervened on their behalf.

THE POWER TEAM MEMBERS FELT A BUMP AT SEVENTY MILES AN HOUR

Perhaps our greatest experience involving divine intervention happened when several members of the Power Team were heading south from Flint, Michigan, on Highway 75 at 7:00 A.M. The team had to get up about three hours earlier to keep a tight schedule after an exhausting crusade the night before. A fifty-five-year-old volunteer driving a fifteen-passenger church van picked them up at the hotel at 6:00 A.M. The team was so tired that all of the men promptly fell back to sleep once the van started moving. Thousands of vehicles zoomed down both sides of this busy six-lane highway, but the exhausted Power Team members were oblivious to the steady stream of traffic.

The van traveled at approximately seventy miles an hour in the middle of the six-lane interstate, when suddenly the slumbering Power Team members were awakened by what felt like a bump, followed by a swerving sensation.

Charter Power Team member Mike Hagen slept in the very back of the van. He remembers feeling the bump and thinking, *Man, I'd better see what happened.* To his horror, he saw the driver of the van slumped over the steering wheel. The cruise control was activated, and the van continued to race ahead.

There was nothing the men could do—even though they were extraordinarily strong professional athletes. The driver's unconscious body was lodged between them, the steering wheel, and the brake. The van barreled directly toward a giant steel pole!

If they hit that steel pole while traveling at that speed, they all would be killed. Road Manager Brandon Hensley, who was lying in the seat directly behind the driver, attempted to climb over the man's slumped-over body to take control. The man was positioned so that Brandon couldn't reach the wheel or the pedals. The van crashed into a fence, went through a deep ditch, then went up, and then down a steep embankment before it crashed into another fence, crossed a field, and ran into the mailbox of a farmhouse. Finally Brandon was able to reach the controls and stop the van.

THIS VAN SHOULD HAVE FLIPPED OVER TWENTY TIMES!

As soon as the van came to a stop, the Power Team members quickly removed the driver from the van and tried to revive him with CPR. It became clear that the man had died and was in the presence of the Lord. When the state police arrived on the scene and investigated the accident, they told Mike Hagen and the other Power Team members, "It is physically impossible for this van to still be in one piece! This van should have flipped over twenty times or run into oncoming traffic." He shook his head in disbelief. "This is a miracle!"

When the people who lived in the farmhouse came out to see what had happened, they were shocked by what they discovered. Of the millions of people who passed by their house on the interstate highway each year traveling to and from such heavily populated areas, they *recognized* our volunteer driver. The house owner told the team members, "I know that man. I just sold him a truck only three days ago!"

The Power Team sensed that God was at work—even in such a bizarre incident. They took the opportunity to invite the man and his entire family to the crusade meeting scheduled for that evening. One of the young men who lived in the house decided to accept the invitation and come to the crusade. That same night he gave his heart to Jesus Christ.

God sent an angel to steer that speeding van to safety to spare the lives of the Power Team members. It was the driver's time to go to heaven, but I believe God even used this man's life and passage into His glory to save yet another precious soul.

Never underestimate the power of God. He is completely able to intervene in any situation, but He often does it in inconceivable ways that we would never anticipate.

He is able to do "immeasurably more than all we ask or imagine, according to his power that is at work within us" (Eph. 3:20).

CONQUER THE
GIANT OF
HARASSMENT

Another giant waited for the Power Team when we accepted a brave Christian missionary's invitation to "perform" in Jordan, an ancient nation situated in the Middle East next to Israel. Its inhabitants are 98 percent Muslim, and it is against the law for anyone to conduct Christian evangelistic rallies in that country. Many people have been thrown in prison simply for telling people about Jesus Christ.

God must have supernaturally opened the doors to that country because I am not sure how we were allowed into that Islamic nation. Perhaps the officials relaxed because our Power Team crusades are so unique and entertaining that they don't seem to be "churchy" to non-Christian people. Even so, we could not advertise our "event" because of that nation's strict laws. We were also warned that if we preached the gospel and the word got out, then we and our hosts could be in great danger.

Evidently the kinds of things we do in a typical crusade are very rare in Jordan. I accidentally tore a pectoral muscle while bending an inch-wide steel bar during one of the evening meetings. I went to see a Jordanian doctor. I can still see the puzzled expression on his face as he struggled to understand the reason for my injury!

We started out on the first night with just one hundred and fifty people, but the crowds quickly grew to eight hundred and more. The crowds just kept getting larger, and people received Jesus Christ as Lord and Savior by the hundreds. We had a real problem on our hands.

By the last night of the crusade, news about our unusual "show" and the massive public response reached the national Jordanian news media. They sent their number one female reporter to the crusade with a film camera crew.

IF YOU PREACH TONIGHT, WE ALL COULD BE PUT IN PRISON!

Our host missionary was really brave, but he never dreamed that one of Jordan's most popular television news personalities would show up at the meetings with a film crew! He sought me out before the crusade started that night and told me, "If you preach tonight, we all could be put in prison! In fact, you could be killed, and you could destroy my work as well. I think you had better really pray about what to do tonight."

I had been studying the power of praise in the Bible for several days before all of this came up. I knew that when King Jehosaphat sent the people of God into battle against the combined armies of two powerful enemies in the Old Testament, he told them to march into battle singing God's praises and shouting, "Give thanks to the LORD, for His love endures forever" (2 Chron. 20:21). When the Israelites marched into battle praising God for His unending mercy, their enemies turned upon one another and destroyed themselves.

68

The original Hebrew word for *mercy* means "loyal love," which is very different from the meaning for the English word *mercy*. That means that the ancient Hebrews marched into battle while singing and shouting, "God's love is *too loyal* to let us be destroyed."

Moments before I began to speak to the crowd of Muslim Jordanians, the Spirit of the Lord seemed to say to my heart, "Go ahead and share My gospel with the people." With that strong confirmation in my heart, I began to very carefully preach the good news to that predominantly Muslim crowd. I felt that I shouldn't hold back any good thing from these people, so I preached the truth—that God loves everyone. I told them, "God so loved the world that he gave his one and only Son, that whoever believes in him shall not perish but have eternal life" (John 3:16).

EVEN THE JORDANIAN CAMERA CREW GOT SAVED!

Meanwhile, I watched the film crew follow my every move with their camera. The film rolled, which meant that every word I preached would be broadcast across a nation that put people in jail for witnessing to just one person. The anointing of God was so powerful that night that when I invited people to receive Jesus Christ as their Lord and Savior, we had a huge response—even the Jordanian camera crew got saved!

Right at the end, though, I sensed that the Lord wanted me to do exactly what the Israelites did in the Old Testament. So, I raised both of my hands and shouted directly into the camera, "Praise the Lord, for His mercy endures forever!"

As soon as I shouted those words, the side of the film camera popped open and the undeveloped movie film shot across the room! Since the Jordanian news crew used a color film camera instead of a video camera, the light exposure destroyed all of the film, and they were not able to show it on the national newscast that night!

Through that experience the Lord showed me that when we face harassment or have to walk through a circumstance or situation that seems impossible, we should shout from our hearts, "Praise the Lord, for His love is too loyal to let us be destroyed!" God will supernaturally move in power and might to deliver us.

David had to face this kind of situation too. When he killed Goliath, he earned the undying hatred of Goliath's four giant brothers. We know that when brother number one showed up shouting threats of discouragement, God defeated him with His faithfulness. When evil brother number two appeared with threats of destruction, God brought him down through His supernatural intervention.

Goliath's third evil brother also showed up during a battle with the Philistines later in David's life. The Bible says, "In another battle with the Philistines at Gob, Elhanan son of Jaare-Oregim the Bethlehemite killed Goliath the Gittite, who had a spear with a shaft like a weaver's rod" (2 Sam. 21:19).

The Bible isn't saying that Elhanan killed Goliath for a second time. The style of the day was at times to use the family name to refer to all of the person's descendants. This verse doesn't mention the name of Goliath's third brother, but the Bible does tell us this giant's name in the book of First Chronicles, which describes the same battle:

> In another battle with the Philistines, Elhanan son of Jair killed Lahmi the brother of Goliath the Gittite, who had a spear with a shaft like a weaver's rod. (1 Chron. 20:5)

In the original Hebrew *Lahmi* means "to harass"! The devil and his crew love to harass us by bringing up our failures, shortcomings, or weaknesses from the past. If that doesn't work, then he will bring up the failures of our parents or of other key people in our lives. He will do anything to hang a rope of failure and unworthiness around our necks so he can drag us down onto his level.

WE WILL ALL HEAR THAT TAUNTING VOICE

God tells us in His Word, "Everyone who wants to live a godly life in Christ Jesus will be persecuted" (2 Tim. 3:12). That means that everyone who takes a stand for Jesus can count on running into a "Lahmi," or a giant of harassment, along the way. We will all hear that taunting voice say things like, "You are weak. You are going to fail because that is what you have always done! Who are you to say you are a Christian—just look at all of your failures! God could never accept you. Your father was an alcoholic, your grandfather was a failure, your whole life has just been one big failure—get used to it."

Sometimes we suffer harassment over things that happened to us during childhood, things that planted fear deep inside our beings or brought physical impairment or sickness. One time I spoke to a large congregation in Florida when I sensed what has to be one of the strangest "leadings" I have ever received from the Lord! I am a conservative, Southern Baptist evangelist who likes to stick to the biblical basics of the gospel, but this time God took me way out on a limb.

While I spoke, I sensed the Spirit of the Lord tell me, "There is a woman in the service who has a bat in her blood." I couldn't help but question this one. I asked the Lord in silent prayer, "Lord, what do You mean by *a bat*?" Instantly, I just "knew" that the Spirit referred to the kind of bat that flies. This kind of leading is only given to God's ministers when He wants to help someone and build the faith of His people. I knew I was supposed to mention this message publicly. The worst thing that could happen was that I would look like a fool. I already knew what that felt like.

THERE IS A WOMAN HERE WHO HAS A BAT IN HER BLOOD

I stepped up in front of two thousand people and said, "I don't really understand this, but I believe the Lord is saying there is a woman here who has a bat in her blood. If you'll come forward, God will set you free." The audience looked at me like I was out of my mind, and I don't blame them.

Suddenly a woman rushed toward the platform from the back of the church screaming, "It's me! It's me!" When she reached the platform, I called her up. She told the audience, "When I was a little girl, some neighborhood boys held me down so they could tease me with a bat that they had killed. While they were teasing me, a drop of the bat's blood somehow got in my mouth. Ever since then, for twelve years, I have suffered from a blood disease I contracted from that dead bat."

After the woman finished her explanation, I prayed for her in the name of Jesus. It was later confirmed that God had healed her of the blood disease. No matter what the enemy uses to harass God's people, there is mercy and grace waiting to bring victory.

The harassing spirit Satan sends to badger God's people especially likes to bring up weak points and past failures. As always, God has His own champion ready to bring down Satan's giant. In David's day, He used a champion named Elhanan, another member of David's band of mighty men. in In Hebrew Elahnan's name means "the mercy of God" or "shelter of grace." God still sends His mercy and grace to bring down the giants of harassment that try to block our way. The Bible says: "Because of his great love for us, God, who is rich in mercy, made us alive with Christ even when we were dead in transgressions [wrongdoing]" (Eph. 2:4–5).

This is exciting to me: Jesus didn't just die for your sins, He died for your weaknesses too. You may be thinking, *What is John saying? I have never heard that in church.*

The prophet Isaiah prophesied about Jesus Christ about seven hundred years before He was born. "But he was wounded for our transgressions, / He was bruised for our iniquities; / The chastisement of our peace was upon Him, / And with His stripes we are healed" (Isa. 53:5 KJV). When the prophet says Jesus was wounded for our transgressions, he described the way Jesus was beaten, nailed to the cross, and pierced with a spear. It was through these wounds that He shed His blood so our sins could be washed away.

When Isaiah says, "He was *bruised* for our iniquities," we have to really think about what he was talking about. What did he mean by "bruised"? What is a bruise? It is a wound, a place of injury where our bodies bleed on the inside. The word *iniquity* means "weakness to a sin." In other words, Jesus bled on the inside for our weakness to sin.

IS THERE A GENETIC WEAKNESS OF THE SOUL?

Have you ever heard anyone say, "The sins of the fathers will be passed down to the children of the third and fourth generation"? That person misquoted a Scripture in the Bible. The verse doesn't actually say sins. I found six places in the Bible that say "the *iniquities* of the forefathers will be passed down to the second, third, and fourth generation."

This is really important: In the same way your parents passed down genetic material that determined what you look like, they can also pass down *weaknesses of the soul* toward certain sins. Thanks to

Jesus Christ, this is not a sentence of doom, but it does explain why some of us have weaknesses toward certain addictions such as alcohol, sexual sins, fear, or pride.

I talked with a lady whose fourteen-year-old daughter had tried to kill herself four times. I looked at her and sensed that I should ask her a very unusual question. "Ma'am, how old were *you* when you first tried to kill yourself?"

She didn't even blink. She instantly told me, "Oh, I was thirteen." We traced that particular weakness toward suicide back for *six generations*! Once this woman knew the source of the problem, she knew the battle had already been won through God's mercy.

The only way you can pass down the weaknesses in your soul to your children is if you let the weaknesses stay there. The good news of Jesus Christ covers all iniquities, even those passed down from generation to generation. Not only was Jesus wounded for your transgressions (which means He "bled on the outside" for your sins to be forgiven), but He was also bruised for your iniquities (which means He "bled on the inside" so your inner weaknesses could be turned into strengths).

WELCOME TO THE ROUGHEST SCHOOL IN AMERICA

Several years ago, someone asked the Power Team to do an assembly at what many people called "the roughest school in America." This school was in the heart of the Bronx, one of the most dangerous boroughs in New York City. We faced an uphill battle the whole way. In fact, the school officials told us they never had whole-school assemblies because they were afraid a riot would break out.

The principal of the school had to hire thirteen fully armed police officers to patrol the school during school hours just to keep the peace. Everyone who wanted to enter the school building had to pass through metal detectors manned by armed guards. Even these security measures failed to stop the violence. I still remember walking down one of the halls in that school building and seeing the outline of a body drawn on the floor. I was told that the police had made the outline while investigating the murder of a boy who had been stabbed there three days earlier. This school in the Bronx had a long history of hopelessness, violence, and fear.

God intervened so that we could hold the school assembly anyway. Before I began the message, I had promised the students in the assembly that I would have policemen come up to the stage and handcuff me. Then I promised them that I would break those cuffs right in front of them.

When we did the feats of strength that day, we managed to capture the attention of those students. I talked to them about overcoming their past to *make a difference*. I challenged them to become dream-makers instead of dream-breakers. At the end of my message I shouted, "Are there any students left here who want to make this world a better place?"

Logically, that seems like a stupid thing to say in a school where every fourth student was a known drug dealer. I didn't care because God had spoken to my heart to challenge the status quo.

I also told the crowd that drug dealers are not heroes. I said, "Don't be impressed with their chains, their hot cars, or pretty girl-friends. In five years they will be dead, in prison, or wasting away in a crack house." The students knew I told the truth. Finally, I said, "Is there anybody who is willing to stand up for what is right?"

THOSE ARE MY CHAINS—
BREAK THEM FOR ME!

At the end of my message, the number one drug dealer in the high school stood when the policeman walked to the stage and handcuffed me. As soon as my hands were bound, he boldly walked down the bleacher stairs and across the gym floor to stand before me. Then, in front of every student in that high school, he screamed at me, "Man, *those are my chains*. Those are *my chains* you're breaking! Now break them for me."

Up to that point, there had been no altar call. When this young man interrupted the assembly to say those words, it so touched the heart of that student body that two thousand students suddenly bolted out of their seats to stand in front of me with this drug dealer. When I snapped the handcuffs, all of the students standing there knew those handcuffs represented the chains around their hearts. They cried, they shouted, and they cheered because they knew they had new lives.

The young people in that tough high school in the Bronx needed to know that they could break out of the bondage of the past. Through Jesus Christ, they could receive the power to break out of "the way things have always been" and reach out for a new future, based on God's ability, instead of their inability! The Lord showed me that if He could make a miracle happen in one of the roughest schools in America, then He *could* take back this generation for God!

The next time the harasser says, "You are weak, just look at your father—he failed. Look at your lousy life—there is no hope." You tell him, "Satan, God's Word shows me that you are a five-time loser. It also tells me that by the wounds of Jesus, I am saved. And the bruises of Jesus have changed all of my inner weaknesses into strengths. I didn't say that—God said it. So take it up with Him."

Consider this: Every time you receive a victory over a particular weakness toward sin, you are winning a victory for more than just yourself. You are winning a victory for the generations to come. Your children and your children's children will be blessed because you chose to stand in God's mercy instead of yielding to Satan's giant of harassment.

GOD IS NEVER CAUGHT OFF GUARD BY THE ENEMY

Don't let the devil harass you with your weaknesses. Jesus paid the price on the cross, so give them to Him forever. God isn't surprised by your weaknesses. Nothing is hidden from Him. He just loves you in spite of your downfalls!

We are *all* weak in the flesh, but God is *never* caught off guard by the enemy's plans and schemes to tempt you. He prepares His mercy beforehand as well.

Several years ago, we had a creative team working on a new edition of the *Power Team Comic Book*. For some reason everyone working on the project felt a sense of urgency. This issue of the comic book dealt with satanism, the occult, and the way these things were beginning to entrap teenagers through demonic computer role-playing games. The general public didn't know about the Internet at this time, but almost prophetically, the writer and artist portrayed teenagers in the plot who unknowingly interacted with satanic leaders through a role-playing game on phone-linked computers.

The topic wasn't considered "politically correct" because it openly dealt with certain aspects of the devil's dark kingdom that many Christians want to hide or dismiss. We knew that the comic book could arouse some powerful opposition from groups that are deeply involved in satanic rituals, the occult, and certain occult role-playing games. Ruthanne and I felt strongly, though, that we needed to deal with the topic. So I told the creative team to keep on working on it.

The writer and the artist didn't know our traveling schedule, but after prayer, they decided to have the plot take place in a fictitious coastal city in Oregon. This would play a crucial role in future events.

The creative crew rushed the production schedule ahead, and the comic books came off the press and were shipped overnight to the Power Team for their very next crusade—*in a coastal city in Oregon.*

THAT NIGHT NEO-PAGANS PLANNED TO ENCIRCLE THE AUDITORIUM!

Only the Lord knew that on that very night an alliance of Neo-Pagan groups from the area planned to encircle the auditorium where the Power Team was scheduled to conduct the evangelistic crusade. The protesters allegedly included members of a local witch coven and some Wiccans.[11]

The protesters held their anti-Christian rally exactly as they planned, but they failed to shut down the crusade. They didn't even limit the size of the crowd—the auditorium was packed to capacity that night, even though people had to walk through the picket lines to get in. When the people left the auditorium after the crusade, thousands of them carried in their hands a colorful Power Team comic book titled *Agents of Death*. It described God's dramatic defeat of an evil plot hatched by a fictitious satanist ring through the power of His risen Son, Jesus Christ!

The enemy had hatched a plot to harass the ministry of the Power Team in hopes of shutting down the preaching of the gospel, but God was too loyal to us to allow the enemy's plot to succeed. God was ahead of Satan all the way, and He had already prepared a spiritual weapon in that comic book for the destruction of the devil's carefully laid plan! We are still amazed at the timing involved in it all. God's mercy once again defeated the giant of harassment the enemy sent to block our way.

Don't let harassment and false claims of the enemy shake your confidence in God. Always put your trust in what God says about you. When the enemy tries to bring up old dead things from the past to keep you down, fill your mind with what God's Word says about you *today*. This is what God has to say about the matter, and His Word is final: "There is therefore now no condemnation to those who are in Christ Jesus" (Rom. 8:1 NKJV). That includes *you*.

You can always count on this fact: God will never harass you. Only Satan stoops that low. *God is rich in mercy, and that is His perfect antidote and weapon to defeat the giant of harassment.* This is the sixth key principle for becoming the Ultimate Champion. His mercy is more than enough to make you strong in every situation. The God inside you is greater than every giant the five-time loser sends your way!

Triumph over the Giant "Self" of Humanism

Several years ago the Power Team traveled to the island of Crete, just off the mainland of Greece. We followed our hosts to the City Square, where the townspeople had constructed a makeshift speaker's platform with bricks.

I preached a brief message, performed some power feats, and asked some local residents to handcuff me with police handcuffs. I didn't know it at the time, but a group of pirates, well-known to everyone in that town, had come ashore and joined the crowd while I preached. These modern-day pirates made a living by raiding and harassing the shipping trade in that region. They were very self-confident and seemed to fear neither man nor God.

Once I was handcuffed, the pirates quickly moved in closer as if by a prearranged signal. There were nearly a thousand people on the square pressing in around me by this time, but the pirates filtered through the crowd toward the makeshift platform until they surrounded me.

I pointed out to the crowd that the handcuffs around my wrists represented the chains that bind our hearts and lives. I would snap the handcuffs to represent the way Jesus Christ completely breaks the chains that bind us. I could sense the power of God in that crowded city square. When I gave the altar call, I had the unforgettable privilege of watching every one of the pirates humbly bow their heads and give their hearts to Jesus!

Until the moment those Cretan pirates bowed their heads in submission to God, their presence in the local waters and in that city represented a constant threat to the public well-being. They were lawless and defiant until they encountered Jesus Christ, the Savior sent as our supreme gift from God.

David also knew what it was like to live under a constant threat of violence and fear. Not only had he lived for years under Saul's constant death threats, but he also went to sleep each night for many years after defeating Goliath wondering if he would meet one of the giant's angry brothers in mortal combat.

THE LAST GIANT:
A LIVING DEATH THREAT TO DAVID

Nowhere in the Bible are we told the name of Goliath's fourth brother, but this last giant represented a living death threat to David and his destiny on the earth. I've discovered that the evil spirit that operated through Goliath's fourth brother is just as dangerous to us today!

> In still another battle, which took place at Gath, there was a huge man with six fingers on each hand and six toes on each foot—twenty-four in all. He also was descended from Rapha. When he taunted Israel, Jonathan son of Shimeah, David's brother, killed him.

These four were descendants of Rapha in Gath, and they fell at the hands of David and his men. (2 Sam. 21:20–22)

This giant had six fingers on each hand and six toes on each foot. Six, six, six, and six. Do you know what this giant represents? He represents the "number of man" marked by self-seeking, self-pleasing, self-exalting behavior, and humanist attitudes.[12] We will all come face to face with this spirit at least once in our lives.

This "no name, all fame" spirit taunts the corporate kingdom of God like all of the other members of Goliath's family, but it has a much deadlier way of approaching us individually. This wily spirit likes to whisper in our ears, "Look at you! Just look at what you've done. Look at what you can do, and who you are! Hey, you deserve better than that."

HOW THE HUMANIST SPIRIT WORMS ITS WAY INTO YOUR HEART

There is an element of sophistication and shrewd manipulation in this fourth giant that doesn't show up in any of the other giants that come our way. It won't bellow and charge you from the front because it is too smart for that. This evil spirit mimics its master Satan when it tries to worm its way into your heart and mind with flattering words and thoughts. It uses "self" words like *me, I, me, mine, you,* and *yours.* This clever spirit from hell has practically succeeded in tricking this entire generation and others into saying, "I am god!"

Perhaps you have recognized this giant as the ancient spirit of humanism and pride. This deceptive, slick-tongued spirit has infected our nation's schools and many of our churches with the "Man is god, I am god" syndrome of secular humanism. He wants to infect every one of us with the deadly virus of pride, which is the same sin that got Satan thrown out of heaven.

I immediately think of the color red every time someone comes up to me and says, "Well, John, your ministry has really grown. You must be reaching millions of people every year. Aren't you proud of what you have accomplished?"

Red comes to mind because someone once told me, "The higher the monkey climbs the tree, the more his ugly red behind shows." The point may be a little crude, but it drives home just how foolish it is for us to brag or take credit for accomplishments to win the respect of other people.

Every time we climb to a higher level of responsibility and public recognition, the more our little mistakes and ugly demeanors show up to those below us. So accomplishments, pro-motion, and acclaim shouldn't flatter us; instead, they should make us even more careful. The higher we climb the tree of responsibility and achievement for God, the more potential we have to hurt people by causing them to stumble through our pride or self-promotion.

Having an egocentric attitude is just the same as saying, "Look, I am God."

Our churches are filled with millions of beautiful, attractive, and productive people who say, "To God be the glory, great things He has done," while in their hearts and minds they are really saying, "We have charisma. Just look at the great things we have done. Success is our name, and business is our game. We like the fact that we are skilled at manipulation. We know how to argue our points, land the big deal, and get the job done."

There are too many self-promoting Christians who worship God in "the house that man built" while smiling to themselves say-ing, "Man, I'm good." The truth is that any time we allow ourselves to think this way, we are setting ourselves up for a fall just like Goliath's fourth brother.

PRIDE: THE ONLY SIN
THAT TOTALLY REPELS GOD

The Bible makes it clear that God's way runs in the opposite direction from the way of the proud. Human pride is the only sin that totally repels God. As I said before, God has never used a proud person to exemplify His glory in the Bible. Pride completely blocks God's access to our hearts, and our access to His love, wisdom, and power.

Human pride is the fuel of "man-centered religion," but pride is the opposite of true salvation by grace. When we repent of our sins and surrender our lives, God runs to us. When we are prideful, it actually causes God to turn His back on us.

We need to strip ourselves of the "stinkin' thinkin'" that leads us to say, "Look what *I*'ve done! Oh yes, I give God the glory, but I sure like to look the way I look!" No, we need to return to the basic truth that we are nothing more than sinners saved by grace. I like what Billy Graham said to a national television audience on *Larry King Live*. He said, "I'm a worm saved by grace."

ALL OF US ARE EQUALLY SINFUL

We know God gave each of us certain talents and abilities, but we like to compare ourselves to one another to feed our pride. It doesn't matter to God where we rank in the looks or abilities department, because all of us are equally sinful in His sight outside of the cross of Jesus Christ. Our ugly side shows when we climb above the crowd to shout our own praise.

God isn't against individuality—He created each of us to be unique and different in certain ways. He simply hates pride because He knows it acts like a cancer on the human heart and on society. Every good gift and natural ability we possess comes from the Father of lights—even the "power to get wealth" comes from Him (James 1:17; Deut. 8:18). In other words, it is all God and not us. The more we put confidence in our own flesh and climb the tree of pride, the more we're going to expose our weaknesses and fail in the end.

The good news is that God has a champion ready to meet and defeat the spirit of Goliath's fourth brother when he shows up in our lives and ministries. The Bible tells us that David's own nephew, Jonathan, killed the giant with six digits who was the last brother in Goliath's house. In the Hebrew, Jonathan's name means "given by God." We should never try to fight our battles with giants using our own strengths or abilities—we need to run to the battle equipped with God.

Jesus tells us, "If you humble yourself, then I will exalt you. When I open a door for you, no man can shut it—no matter what earthly title they may have" (adapted from Matt. 23:12; Rev. 3:8). If you take care of your relationship with Jesus, then He'll take care of everything else in your life (Matt. 6:33).

We are living in a season of giants today. This is a season when God wants to put a fresh anointing on every one of us. Unfortunately, I am convinced that nearly 85 percent of the Christians in America will remain the same spiritually, unless something drastic happens. We have become so complacent, comfortable, and satisfied in our salvation rockers that we have lost our urgent sense of destiny. We have lost sight of the fact that God put us here to make a difference. He created us to be world-shakers and history-makers for Him, but you would never know it. It only takes one person who is totally sold out to God to turn the tide of history!

TELECOMICUS LEFT HIS GARDEN FOR THE GLADIATOR RING

I remember hearing the story about a monk named Telecomicus who lived in a monastery in Europe about seventeen hundred years ago, during the reign of the Roman emperor Constantine. All Telecomicus did for most of his adult life was work in the garden and pray. He was short, and he had no hair.

One day while he worked in the monastery garden, God spoke to him: "Telecomicus, go to Rome."

The monk hadn't been outside the monastery since he was a young man. He replied, "Lord, is that really You?"

Telecomicus felt so impressed in his heart to go to Rome that he put up his gardening tools, told his brothers of his mission, and left the monastery cloister to begin his journey to Rome. When he finally arrived in Rome, he still didn't know what God wanted him to do or where he should go. He noticed, however, a large crowd of people hurrying toward a large amphitheater in the center of the city, so he decided to follow them.

The monk had no idea what he would see inside the massive arena. He followed the flow of people into the amphitheater and made his way to the very top seats in the structure. Just then two gladiators entered.

The Bloodthirsty Crowd Roared Its Approval

With a rush of violent fury, the gladiators came together cutting, slashing, and smashing one another with balls and chains, swords, spiked shields, and clubs. Finally one of the gladiators killed the other while the bloodthirsty Roman crowd roared its approval. Telecomicus was nearly in shock at this spectacle. Appalled by the brutality of the bloody contest, he was sickened by the cheers of the crowd over the impending death of another person.

John at his best as he delivers
an inspiring message of hope.

Ruthanne and Trey Jacobs are enthralled as John delivers
a powerful and moving message at a crusade.

Longtime Power Team member and loyal friend Mike Hagen snaps the chains of oppression.

John with Larry Jones, president and founder of Feed the Children.

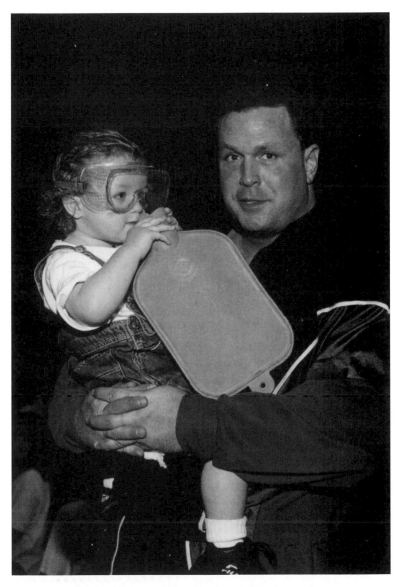

John and his son, John Jacobs III (Trey)—perhaps
a future Power Team member.

Giant billboard in London, England, advertising a Power Team crusade.

Hundreds wait in line to see the Power Team in Victoria, Texas.

At a Power Team crusade, world-renowned actor Chuck Norris shares his testimony about what God has done in his life.

During a crusade in Tucker, Georgia, "Big James" Henderson embraces his spiritual duty by conducting a baptism.

John with eight-time Mr. Olympia (bodybuilding champion), Lee Haney.

In the early days of the Power Team—John is locked in two pairs of handcuffs as the Power Team pulls each side, breaking the chains for future generations.

Veteran Power Team member Berry Handley crushes the "walls of sin."

The Power Team with John as he breaks the chains into the twenty-first century and tears down Satan's walls.

Power Team member Aaron Bell snaps a Louisville Slugger bat as part of a message designed to break the devil's stronghold over today's youth.

The Power Team prays together before going on stage for the *Walker, Texas Ranger* shoot.

John and Pastor Perry Sanders (pictured at top right) pray over the hundreds who just accepted Jesus Christ at a crusade in Lafayette, Louisiana.

Finally, he had seen more than he could bear. Telecomicus jumped up from the stone bench and began to scream with all of his strength, "In the name of God, stop! In the name of God, stop!"

At first the people around Telecomicus laughed at him, pushed him, and spit in his face. Overwhelmed with godly passion, though, the monk began to force his way through the drunken crowds, running down the steps toward the arena floor. "In the name of God, stop!"

Meanwhile, a second pair of gladiators met in the center of the arena. One wielded a doubled-edged battle-ax. His opponent fought with a spiked ball and chain. Telecomicus was only halfway down to the bottom when one of the gladiators cut off his opponent's head. Once again, the crowd roared with approval.

While the monk continued crying out and struggling to reach the bottom level, two more gladiators stepped out onto the blood-splattered dirt floor of the massive stone arena. Finally, Telecomicus managed to reach the bottom level of the stadium. Without hesitation or forethought, the monk quickly climbed over the barricade and ran into the middle of the arena floor. He placed his body between the approaching gladiators. He held up both of his hands and screamed out with all the fervor he could muster, "In the name of God, stop! In the name of God, stop! In the name of God, stop!"

The Gladiator Ran His Spear Through Telecomicus's Frail Body

The same crowd that only moments earlier had laughed, mocked, elbowed, and spit at him, now became eerily quiet. For some reason, the crowd admired this man. Perhaps it was his courage; perhaps it was his passion. Whatever this man stood for, the passion in his eyes and heart began to communicate to the hardened hearts of the people.

The monk frantically held up his hands and waved them at the crowd as he shouted, "In the name of God, stop!" In that moment, one of the gladiators approached Telecomicus and ran his spear all the way through the man's frail body.

The battle-hardened gladiator lifted the monk's body high in the air and slammed him down to the floor of the arena using a move that had always been a crowd-pleaser. As Telecomicus lay there with his body quivering and his blood mingling with the blood of thousands of other victims in the soil of that arena, he still uttered the words, "In the name of God, stop!"

A miracle had happened in the midst of the tragedy. The courageous self-sacrifice of this gentle monk had somehow changed the heart of the crowd. For reasons they didn't understand, the people now felt only disgust over the senseless murder of such a passionate and defenseless man. The most disgusted ones actually began to file out of the amphitheater, and it caused a chain reaction. People began to leave by the thousands in respect for the little man who had given his life. One man's demonstration of courage changed history forever.

Telecomicus' Brave Death Shamed Emperor Constantine

The events of that day caused such a stir across the Roman Empire that the news even reached Emperor Constantine. Although he had claimed allegiance to Christ, he had been unable to gather the courage to ban the popular gladiator contests. It is said that the brave death of humble Telecomicus shamed Emperor Constantine into issuing a royal decree that banned the Roman tradition of gladiatorial contests.

The significance of this story isn't that one monk managed to stop the gladiators. It was that the courage and faith of Telecomicus *moved God's hand* to change the course of history. What would happen in our day if we dared to stand up to the evil spiritual powers that threaten our kids, schools, and cities? What would happen if we said, "In the name of God, stop!" with the same courage and unyielding determination displayed by Telecomicus? If we dared take action, God would once again be moved to change the course of history.

God looks for people He can use to change the world. He wants to pour out a "giant-killing" anointing on us! Though you may face disappointment, the good news is that God, who is rich in mercy, will show Himself faithful.

God is looking for some people in our churches who are not afraid to pick up their slingshot and say, "Is there not a cause?" God wants to use you, and it is time for you to reclaim your sense of destiny. If you are doing God's will, then you need to realize you cannot lose! I have news for you: No matter where you live, how old you are, or how much schooling you have—God wants to use you to change the world!

With the devil working so hard to steal your sense of destiny, this is not the time to just sit in your favorite church pew and soak in the praise and worship. While He was on this earth, the last thing Jesus said was, "Go and tell" (Matt. 28:19–20).

Now if a soldier gets lost in the battlefield, he is supposed to go back to the last instructions issued by the general and follow those orders until advised otherwise. If you are wondering what you are supposed to do for God, you need to go back to His last instructions on the battlefield. He said, "Go and tell." In other words, "Go do something."

EVERYTHING YOU NEED FOR VICTORY COMES FROM ONE SOURCE

God wants us to have the supernatural anointing we need to pull down every giant who dares come against this generation! Listen, God called us into His kingdom to do more than just grab what we want. He has ordained us to be what we can be and do what we can do for God.

The faithfulness of God killed discouragement. The supernatural intervention of God killed destruction. The mercy of God killed harassment. And the gift of God killed the spirit of humanism.

Everything you need for victory comes from one Source and only one Source. That means that if you want to win, surrender to God. If you try to hang onto your life and your own way of doing things, you are going to lose it all in the end. True fulfillment—the kind that brings satisfaction and joy to every cell of your body—can only come through total surrender to the purposes of God. Every one of us will have to face the giant of self-seeking, self-pleasing, and self-exaltation. The test will come as surely as the sun rises in the east. We just need to remember that the giant of self was killed by a man named "given by God."

When you surrender everything to Jesus Christ—when you live your life like it no longer belongs to you—you have become the Ultimate Champion. James, the apostle, told us, "Every good and perfect gift is from above, coming down from the Father of the heavenly lights, who does not change like shifting shadows" (James 1:17). The truth in this passage reveals the seventh key principle for becoming an Ultimate Champion:

> Overcome the giant of self by remembering that every good thing comes from God.

THIS GENERATION FACES FAITH-SHAKING GIANTS

The history of Goliath and his four brothers is more than just a story about giants. It is a manual for spiritual warfare. Every giant in Goliath's family represents a spirit that is active and operating in the earth this very moment. The devil hasn't changed, and he hasn't dreamed up anything new since he was thrown out of heaven.

This generation faces the faith-shaking giants of discouragement, destruction, harassment, and self-seeking, self-pleasing humanism. I sometimes wonder if there has ever been a society in history more humanistic than ours. Ancient Rome may have come close, but I think we have even moved beyond their wretched mark.

God's answer to the giants in our lives is far-reaching. For instance, the principles of victory over the giant "self" of humanism even brings success in the areas of giving and finances. My grandparents died and went to heaven several years ago, and they left me four hundred acres of swampland on which we hunt and fish. I appreciated the land, but it wasn't worth anything to anyone else because you couldn't plant crops on the land, and you couldn't even harvest the trees that were already there.

The day came when Ruthanne and I received word that a minister and his family were in serious financial trouble. This man served the Lord faithfully doing missions work all over the world, and the Lord spoke to me to send that family a large sum of money. My first response was to reply to the Lord in prayer, "Lord, that would have to come out of the savings we have accumulated over the years because we don't have this kind of money." The very next morning, Ruthanne and I took the money out of savings and sent it to help the minister who had helped so many others across the world, as God had asked us to do.

Two months later I received a phone call from an official with the Department of Fish, Wildlife, and Ecology. "Mr. Jacobs," he said, "we have had a strange phenomenon occur on your swamp land. We have found over one hundred plants that don't grow anywhere else in this hemisphere. Basically, your four hundred acres of worthless swamp land has just become some of the most valuable conservation land in North America."

You Can't Out-Give God!

To make a long story short, the federal government bought the land from me and sent me the largest check I had ever seen! I learned that you can't out-give God because He will always answer your faith with even greater blessings.

I feel that God is saying to the Church, "Wake up, mighty men! Wake up, mighty women! It is time for war; it is the season of giants. Will you dare to follow me into battle?"

The mighty men who killed Goliath's brothers didn't start out as superstars or great warriors. David's mighty men began as disgruntled, disheartened men who were outcasts saddled with crushing debt and a deficit of hope. In one of the lowest points in David's life, God sent him four hundred men who felt even lower than he did. Then God anointed David to give those men a sense of destiny. He taught them to believe that in God they could not fail. They *could* change the world! Those men became giant-killers who helped David change the world.

The Church needs that same giant-killing sense of destiny today!

ARE YOU READY TO GO TO THE NEXT LEVEL?

A high school assembly seemed to be going well for a member of the Power Team until a young student suddenly interrupted the meeting. He stood up and boldly extended both of his hands toward the stage. A pentagram—a five-pointed star used as an occult symbol—had been tattooed on the palms of both hands. The Team member immediately understood why he had seen thirty or forty students dressed like witches and warlocks. (We run into this kind of thing more often than you could imagine.)

The Power Team member was a seasoned minister of the gospel, so he refused to be intimidated by the young man's devilish stunt. He delivered a passionate "nonreligious" message to his audience of teenagers and challenged them to make their lives count. Then he told them it *was* possible to overcome the past and do what is right.

A girl came up to him after the assembly and bluntly told him that she was a witch, and that her mother was also a witch. She said she was one of the leaders of the witchcraft group operating in that high school.

After the Power Team member talked with the girl for ten minutes, the love of Jesus that was evident in his life softened her heart. He was able to present the gospel to her. She immediately said, "I want to know Jesus. I want to pray right now." She fell to her knees and prayed the sinner's prayer with him right there in the gym, even though some of her friends watched! She looked up with tears streaming down her cheeks and said, "Now, what can I do for God?" He simply told her, "Invite your whole school to the Power Team crusade."[13]

INTRODUCED TO JESUS AND
SET FREE FROM WITCHCRAFT

Little did we dream that later that night sixty students from that high school would walk forward to receive Jesus Christ in our Power Team crusade! When we asked the students how they ended up at the crusade, they said, "Are you kidding? Some girl went running up and down the hallways of the school shouting, 'Come see the Power Team! They introduced me to Jesus and set me free from witchcraft.'"

The bold public testimony and transformation of this former teenage witch caused such a stir in the school that the students came out by the hundreds to see what happened!

I call what happened to this young girl a "day and night" transformation. Such transformations are more common than you would think, especially if you take the gospel into the lives of the lost, where it is needed. We were conducting a Power Team crusade in a football stadium in Columbus, Ohio, when a teenage girl came up to me carrying a cute one-year-old boy all dressed up in blue-jean overalls and a little baseball cap.

The girl said, "John Jacobs, do you see my baby?"

I said, "Yes."

"You spoke at my school a year and a half ago. I was sixteen and pregnant, but nobody knew about it but me, my boyfriend, and his parents. The day you came to my school, I had promised my boyfriend's parents that I was going to have an abortion."

The girl glanced at her little boy, then she looked at me. "You encouraged me and all of my friends that day to come back to see the Power Team that night, the same time I was scheduled to have the abortion. I went to the Power Team crusade instead of having the abortion. I got saved that night, and I dumped my boyfriend—not the baby." She held up her little son and said with tears in her eyes, "This is the baby."

According to the world—and especially this girl's boyfriend and his parents—it would have been easier all around if she had aborted that baby. The problem is that it is wrong to kill a baby for the sake of personal convenience or selfishness. I didn't save that little baby boy, I just happened to be the person God used that particular night. It was the life-changing, life-transforming power of Jesus Christ that gave that young mother the courage to do the right thing.

DON'T BE CONTENT TO SCROUNGE FOR HANDOUTS AT THE DOOR OF HEAVEN

God is calling the Church—you and me—*to go to the next level.* It is too easy for us to live with the same bad habits, the same insecurities, and the same shortcomings that have plagued our lives for decades. We tend to go only so far with God, and then we stop. We learn to be content scrounging for handouts at the door of heaven instead of entering in to join the family feast at the Lord's table! Enough is enough. It is time to get up and move on in Jesus' name.

It is impossible to please God when you are content to live in the passionless realm of mediocrity and apathy. We need a passionate hunger for more of God and less ego. If you are sincere, He will show up in your life with more than you've ever dreamed!

Most people don't like change. We fear taking the risks involved in discarding the old to reach out for the new things God has for us. That leaves us with only one alternative: to learn how to live with our sins and failures. God never asked us to do that!

THE MOST POPULAR EXCUSE

Have you ever heard someone say, "Well, I'm German (or Italian or Irish), so I have a hot temper"? No matter what nationality or ethnic group uses this universal excuse, they believe one thing to be true: *That's just the way I am.* This really means, "I am a sinner, and I don't want to change."

Have you ever heard this: "I just worry all the time—it's just me"?

I often hear Christian men add their own twist to the excuse game when they say, "Well, every Christian man I know struggles with lust. At least I'm not gay."

What we are really saying is, "I've learned to live with my sins and failures. I've learned how to put up with my wrong desires because it is easier than letting God change me." It scares me to think what would happen if those "wrong desires" we put up with began to threaten the lives and futures of our children because we failed to put them under our feet!

God doesn't want us to put up with our faults. He wants us to allow Him to break them forever by taking us up to the next level. With no obstacle or spiritual pollution there to block the full downpour of God's blessing, He wants to open heaven's door for us to receive his abundant glory.

This will never happen unless we develop a driving passion to press into God's presence. It is this kind of passion that causes Him to supernaturally "zap us" and lift us to the next level.

Relay races rank among my favorite Olympic events because I like to watch the runners pass the baton. Everything seems to hinge on their success or failure to "pass on the vision" to the next man. No matter how fast or famous the members of a relay team may be, if they fumble the baton, they will lose the race. The same is true in the spiritual race.

The Church is fumbling with God's baton. We are either passing on a counterfeit baton to our children and grandchildren or completely dropping God's baton. The divorce rate in the Church is no different from the divorce rate in the world. Church youth groups across America are riddled with fornication, drugs, alcohol abuse, and open carnality revealed by provocative clothing, immoral joking, and coarse lewdness. These children have inherited their compromised lifestyles from Christian parents who have made careers out of "learning how to live with sin."

A NEW DAY FOR BATON FUMBLERS

The wrong thinking, weak morals, and sinful habits we pass down to our children grow worse with every generation. It won't take long for this kind of vicious cycle to kill and destroy the dreams and the future of our children. Yet, even with all of our baton fumbling, I am encouraged. The Lord is at work in our lives, and He reminds me that this is a *new day*.

All my life I've heard Christian teachers teach that we are transformed and changed gradually as we grow in knowledge. There is a place for growing in knowledge and maturity, but *transformation* only comes when God "zaps" you with His life-changing power. When He touches your life, change will be anything but gradual!

The Bible is filled with accounts of average men who changed the world and became heroes of faith. Do you know what most of these men had in common? They could point to *a certain day* in their lives when they got sick of themselves and said, "God, I want to see Your glory. Touch my life and lift me up. I am not going to let go of you until you bless me." They wrestled with God and with themselves until they were dramatically and irreversibly changed. I can't explain it all, but I can back it up with the Bible. Perhaps the most dramatic proof of this is in the incredible life of Jacob, who was later called Israel.

JACOB ROBBED HIS BROTHER TWO WAYS

Jacob, the second son of Isaac, really lived up to his name. *Jacob* means "heel-snatcher" or "schemer, trickster, manipulator, and prankster." God ordained Jacob to fulfill a great destiny, but he would never fulfill his true calling without leaving his old ways behind. How many of us are in the same situation right now?

Jacob, the schemer, took his older brother Esau's birthright by deliberately playing on his weaknesses. This was a serious loss in ancient Middle Eastern cultures, because a birthright consisted of the special rights, privileges, and specific possessions reserved for the firstborn male in a household. Jacob stole most of his brother's rightful inheritance with a single bowl of red lentil stew and a piece of bread. This amounted to stealing the family's physical assets and estate from his brother.

By birthright, Esau should have had his father Isaac's final blessing, which is the equivalent of a spiritual last will and testament. Isaac was nearly blind in his final days, and Jacob deliberately lied and used his father's visual impairment to his own advantage by pretending to be Esau. By doing this, Jacob managed to steal Esau's spiritual inheritance.

This is not the description of a "good" man. Yet Jacob is revered today as one of the three great patriarchs of Judaism, and he is a key figure in the coming of the Messiah, Jesus Christ. What happened to change this man from a con into a Bible hero?

Jacob was a man who was destined for greatness by God, but his life should prove that you can be anointed and appointed for greatness and still fall short! However, Jacob's life should also be a warning to you if you are one of the people called by God while still living like a thief and a liar. Your day of reckoning comes quickly. God loves you too much to let you stay the way you are! It is almost inevitable that whatever you have done to others will also be done to you.

THE CON MAN GETS CONNED

Once Esau realized what his younger brother had done, Jacob had to run for his life. He ended up living with and working for a man named Laban on the far side of a desert. When Jacob fell in love with Laban's younger daughter, Rachel, Laban used Jacob's weakness to his own advantage.

Laban promised Jacob he could marry Rachel if he worked for him for seven years. Jacob honored his agreement. After the lengthy Middle Eastern wedding feast, Jacob took his veiled wife home. The next morning he discovered, to his dismay, that the bride lying beside him wasn't Rachel, but her older sister Leah! The con man got conned, and it took another seven-year hitch with Laban before he could marry Rachel.

What you sow, you will reap. If you manipulate, you will be manipulated. If you lie, others will lie to you. If you cheat, you will be cheated. The list is endless, and so is the pain. In the end, Jacob, the trickster, worked for his scheming father-in-law for a total of twenty years before he finally broke out on his own.

Don't feel sorry for him, though. God's hand of correction, blessing, and anointing was on Jacob the whole time. God's favor set up Jacob to go to the next level. Jacob became very rich while working for his father-in-law—even though his father-in-law tried to cheat him at every turn. No matter what happened, Jacob seemed to come out on top. Unfortunately, he still wasn't confident in his own ability to "make the deal" and prosper until *one day* . . .

TIME FOR THE TRICKSTER TO GO
TO ANOTHER LEVEL

One day God told Jacob to return to his native land with his family and all of his possessions. He had a brief confrontation with Laban, but God had already intervened by warning Laban not to harm Jacob or even speak to him.

On the journey home, Jacob learned that his brother Esau was approaching with four hundred men. Naturally Jacob felt a little paranoid. He prayed a desperate prayer to God and divided his family and goods into two groups, hoping that if one group was taken, the other would escape.

Jacob schemed right up to the moment of his transformation. He decided to send a small fortune in money, a large herd of livestock, and a number of servants ahead of him as a "gift" to soften Esau's attitude. Then Jacob prepared for the worst: "That night Jacob got up and took his two wives, his two maidservants and his eleven sons and crossed the ford of the Jabbok. After he had sent them across the stream, he sent over all his possessions. So Jacob was left alone, and a man wrestled with him till daybreak" (Gen. 32:22–24).

So Jacob was *left alone*. The trickster's confidence no longer rested on his ability to manipulate or scheme. His brother already knew about Jacob's tricks from firsthand knowledge. In Jacob's mind, all Esau wanted to do was kill him. He sat by a campfire at a deserted river ford, alone in the night and separated from his family and possessions. The next thing we know, a man shows up to wrestle with Jacob until sunrise.

DESPERATE FOR A CHANGE

The book of Hosea says that Jacob "struggled with the angel" (Hosea 12:4). It seems clear, though, that Jacob actually wrestled with Jesus Christ. This was a man who had hit bottom. He halfway expected Esau to order his band of men to kill every one of his family and servants. He remembered what God had told him about his destiny, but he also knew he wasn't any closer to fulfilling it. He was desperate for a change.

When the man saw that he could not overpower him, he touched the socket of Jacob's hip so that his hip was wrenched as he wrestled with the man. Then the man said, "Let me go, for it is daybreak."

But Jacob replied, "I will not let you go unless you bless me." The man asked him, "What is your name?"

"Jacob," he answered. Then the man said, "Your name will no longer be Jacob, but Israel, because you have struggled with God and with men and have overcome."

Jacob said, "Please tell me your name."

But he replied, "Why do you ask my name?" Then he blessed him there.

So Jacob called the place Peniel, saying, "It is because I saw God face to face, and yet my life was spared." (Gen. 32:25–30)

The Lord knew Jacob was desperate. He set up Jacob with the simple question: "What is your name?" He wanted the schemer to say his name one last time. Once it was said, the Lord changed Jacob, and the course of history, when He said, "Your name will no longer be Jacob, but Israel." *Israel* in Hebrew means "prince of God" or "contender for the Lord." This marked more than just a name change for Jacob—it marked the permanent transformation of his life.

IT'S NOT ME, IT'S ALL GOD

The Key to Going to the Next Level

True transformation begins the moment you lose confidence in your own ability. We have to come to a humble place in our lives before we can even think about moving on to a higher level with God. Then we have to wrestle with ourselves and with God. In our passion to be like Him, we need to cling to the Lord and say, "Lord, I'm not going to let go of You until You change me. I refuse to stay the way I am." This is the eighth key principle for becoming the Ultimate Champion.

Transformation will only come when the sin in your life bothers you so much that you just refuse to put up with it one more day. Frankly, if you are truly born again, any sin bothers you in some way.

There are only a few places in the Bible where people say they actually saw God. Jacob's response to the miracle at the river ford says it all: "I saw God face to face, and yet my life was spared" (Gen. 32:30).

On that *one day* when you come to a humble place in your life, there may be nowhere to hide and no one to run to. But if you dare to pray, "God, I want more of You," I tell you that He will show up. You will experience God's presence as never before. Corporate worship services and prayer times are necessary and wonderful, but there is something special about the alone times when we come to God in humility with a desperate hunger for His presence.

If you wrestle with God alone, in the twilight of your strength, you will be a different person when the sun rises again. Your transformation won't be gradual. The touch of God on a desperate soul brings instant and dramatic results that last for a lifetime.

In Jacob's case, he remained human enough to fail from time to time, but I am not aware of another incident of manipulation or scheming after his transformation. He became the father of the twelve tribes of Israel and the last patriarch of God's chosen nation.

HE THREW HIMSELF ON
HIS FATHER'S GRAVE

Jack was the young pastor of an Independent Baptist congregation of one hundred people. Nothing much ever happened in this church. But *one day* the pastor's father died. Jack's father was still an alcoholic and yet a long-time member of Jack's church at the time of his death. Jack was so bothered by this that at the funeral, he threw himself on his father's grave and began to weep uncontrollably. He prayed, "God, I refuse to stay a *powerless preacher* anymore."

This heart-wrenching scene continued for hours. His family members left, and most of his friends left as well. The few friends who lingered the longest still remember how worried they were when they finally left the gravesite late that night. They said Jack was still crying out in brokenhearted prayer, "God, I refuse to stay a powerless preacher anymore."

When Jack finally pulled himself away from his father's grave thirty-some years ago, he was a changed man. His church started growing the very next day, and it hasn't stopped since. Today, Jack pastors a church with thirty thousand members, arguably the largest church in North America. The man who has been called America's greatest soul winner was transformed in just *one day*.

There was an average shoe salesman living far below his God-given destiny until someone like you bought a pair of shoes. This person didn't worry about the inconvenience or the risk of rejection involved in witnessing to a shoe salesman, so he led the young salesman to Jesus. The salesman's name was Moody—D. L. Moody. He became the Billy Graham of the nineteenth century. You probably recognize the name if you have ever heard of the Moody Bible Institute or listened to a Moody Bible Network program. The ministry of this "saved shoe salesman" still makes a powerful impact on countless lives around the world.

D. L. Moody refused to put up with anything that limited his service to God. *One day* he took out a full-page newspaper ad in Chicago and challenged every atheist in the city to meet him publicly at the Civic Center. Five thousand atheists showed up at the Chicago Civic Center. D. L. Moody gave them his most fiery message. At the end of the message he gave an altar call, and two hundred atheists came forward.

Most of us would be ecstatic about that kind of response from such a hardened crowd, but D. L. Moody was bothered by the fact that "only" two hundred out of five thousand atheists were converted to Christ through his ministry. "Perhaps there was something in my life that has held back or hindered the move of God," he said to himself. Right there in front of the 4,800 atheists who refused to answer the call to Christ, D. L. Moody fell on his face and wept uncontrollably for forty-five minutes. Why? It *bothered him* to think that anything in his life might hold back the move of God.

While D. L. Moody Wept, God Drew Four Thousand More Atheists into the Kingdom

When the evangelist finally stood up, four thousand more atheists had come forward to receive Jesus Christ! While D. L. Moody wept before God, the arm of the Lord moved across that crowd and transformed four thousand sworn enemies into redeemed children of God!

God always shows up when you are passionate enough to cry

out for more of His presence. He always answers when you make up your mind to wrestle with Him in prayer until your life is changed. This is where the glory comes out.

Today is a new day in God. It is time to receive a new anointing from God. Seek Him, cling to Him, and don't let go of Him until He changes you. Ask Him to reveal His glory in your life, in your children, and in your future. Be willing to totally yield to Him. Once you do this, your past will never again hold you back.

Every hero in the Bible shares one thing in common with Jacob: They can point to *one day* in their lives when they got sick of themselves and said, "God, I want to see Your glory. Please touch my life and lift me up. I'm not going to let go of You until You bless me." If you have a *passion* for God and a *passion* to change, then you will see your children's children become world shakers and history makers. When you die to self, you step up to another level.

There Is Hope for "Five-O'clock People"

Certain childhood memories can still bring a twinge of pain at times. In elementary school I was a little uncoordinated and under-developed. I can still remember how it felt to watch every single kid in my class get picked for sports teams—everyone except me. First they picked the guys who could really play, then they picked the rest. Finally they picked the girls one by one. And then there was me. I remember the rejection I felt every time the gym teacher would put her arm around me in front of my class and say, "Come on, who will pick John? Ah, come on!"

I did my best to handle the insecurities and fears. My best just didn't seem to be good enough. My parents had just gotten a divorce, and it was a bitter one. I soon developed a stutter. I wasn't even able to say five words straight. That almost always made my classmates and the neighborhood kids laugh at me.

Since I wasn't coordinated yet, I usually struck out in softball and missed the ball entirely in kick ball. I didn't have a dad around to teach me how to do those things. My only escape was to go fishing every day, a hobby I still believe is very healthy for young boys.

Things started to change the summer I turned nine. I used to watch the high school kids play football in the school playground. One day they called me over and asked me to play. For some reason, they took an interest in me and began to teach me how to catch and throw the football.

Then my dad started to spend some time with me again after he and Mom were divorced. He played catch with me almost every night under the streetlights. It didn't take long for me to see results. I played football in the afternoon and catch every night. Within three months I could throw a football forty-five yards and catch any pass thrown to me. All of a sudden, I had become extremely coordinated and very confident.

When the school year started again in Louisiana, everything changed for me. As soon as my classmates saw me throw the football, I went from getting picked last in every gym class to being picked first.

LORD, PICK ME

My family eventually moved to Indiana to live with my grandparents. I attended my grandparents' church. Then it dawned on me that God wanted me on His team—so much that He sacrificed His own Son. I was so moved by His love that I went forward to the altar to give my heart to Christ, and I said, "Lord, pick me."

This chapter is for every reader who has ever been picked last. Have you ever been put down or made to feel like you are not good enough? Have you ever felt insecure or left out because you couldn't measure up? Have people said things to you that crushed you on the inside? There is hope for you in the gospel of Matthew. Jesus said:

"For the kingdom of heaven is like a landowner who went out early in the morning to hire men to work in his vineyard. He agreed to pay them a denarius for the day and sent them into his vineyard.

"About the third hour he went out and saw others standing in the marketplace doing nothing. He told them, 'You also go and work in my vineyard, and I will pay you whatever is right.' So they went.

"He went out again about the sixth hour and the ninth hour and did the same thing. About the eleventh hour he went out and found still others standing around. He asked them, 'Why have you been standing here all day long doing nothing?'

"'Because no one has hired us,' they answered.

"He said to them, 'You also go and work in my vineyard.'

"When evening came, the owner of the vineyard said to his foreman, 'Call the workers and pay them their wages, beginning with the last ones hired and going on to the first.'" (Matt. 20:1–8)

YOU ARE WORTH THIS MUCH

This passage gives us a portrait of God's heart. He is like a landowner going out early in the morning to hire workers. He is the one who picked you and me and said, "You are worth this much." Then he sent His only Son to pay our price on Calvary. God so loved the world that He paid all He could pay.

Now this landowner kept coming back to find workers four more times that day, long after the "first string" workers, the hard-working, able-bodied, early risers had already been hired and sent into the fields. It didn't matter to him that the only men left in the town square were the slackers who avoided work—the people no one else wanted to hire.

This landowner knew he would only have one chance to bring

in the harvest before it spoiled in the fields. He wasn't looking for rocket scientists, mechanical engineers, or attorneys that morning; he was looking for anyone who was still breathing to help him bring in the harvest.

You can imagine what kind of workers he had to choose from by the eleventh hour (5:00 P.M.). These were the worst of the lot, the bottom of the barrel. If they weren't just plain lazy, then there was some other reason that no one else would hire them. Maybe there were some young men in the group who looked healthy on the outside but were broken on the inside. Perhaps some of them were blind in one eye, were missing an arm or a leg, or were elderly and suffering from crippling arthritis in their hands, knees, or shoulders.

This didn't matter to him. He had a place reserved for them in his fields, a place where their particular abilities were vital to his harvest. When he looked at these rejected and dejected workers, he looked beyond their faults and impairments and saw the potential fruits of the harvest they could bring in from the field.

ONE FIVE-O'CLOCK PERSON HELD THE KEY TO VICTORY

Napoleon Bonaparte of France was one of the greatest generals who ever lived. During one battle, his generals began to report that troops were being overrun and were taking heavy losses on every front. It was their unpleasant duty to tell Napoleon that the French army had to retreat because their forces were being defeated on all sides by a much larger army.

Before the days of the telegraph, telephone, and radio communications, armies marched to the cadence of drums and the sound of bugles. Military leaders actually issued their battle orders through prearranged drum rhythms and bugle calls because it took too long to send couriers to their field commanders in the heat of battle.

Napoleon turned to the drummer boy he kept at his side at all times. The famous general barked the command, "Drummer boy, sound retreat! Sound retreat."

The young drummer didn't move or respond in any way. He just stood there in awe.

Finally Napoleon and two of his generals turned to the boy and the powerful military leader yelled, "Drummer boy! I said, sound the retreat! Now beat retreat on those drums."

The twelve-year-old boy looked up at the great general and said, "Sir, I don't know how to play retreat. No one has ever taught me how to play retreat. I only know how to play charge." Then this little five-o'clock person who only knew how to play one thing on his drum said, "But if you let me play charge, I will rally our men. If you let me play charge, I will inspire the men to turn the tide of this battle."

Let Him Play Charge!

Napoleon looked at his generals, and they said, "What can we do?"

He said, "Let him play charge!"

That little boy began to play the only thing he knew how to play on his drums, but he played charge like no one else could play it. I understand that when the French soldiers heard the sound of their drummer boy play "charge," even when their army was facing certain defeat, they began to fight with ferocity and determination. Within just a few hours, the tide turned! Before the day was out, Napoleon's troops pursued their defeated opponents with the little drummer boy still playing.

The devil doesn't want Christians to know any other tune but the sound of retreat. He wants us to give up on our marriages, our families, our children, and our calling in God. He especially wants us to give up on what God has called us to do in this life.

There is only one cadence of the cross, and that is the drumbeat that signals us to charge into battle, to go forward, to take our stand no matter how bad things look. God will never get tired of picking you up when you fall, but you have to be willing to say, "Lord, here I am."

We serve the God of the five-o'clock people, the Creator who delights in making the weak strong, and transforming throwaways into champions. The God who created the universe with only words—needs just a little—to do a lot.

I love the story of the landowner; it is *my* story. I would have been one of the people sitting there in the town square because no one else was willing to pick me. There are a lot of five-o'clock people in America today. As I said previously, it is estimated that as many as seventy million Americans suffer from depression in one form or another. Perhaps it is because from the time our children are born, they suffer from an excessively competitive love-you-based-on-your-performance lifestyle. I love to compete, but I also know that competitiveness can be taken too far.

I am concerned when I see our young people ranked and separated according to arbitrary tests. Most of our greatest inventors, mathematicians, and writers in the last century probably wouldn't have made the grade with these tests either! God doesn't choose people for their abilities; He chooses them for their passion and potential.

FROM HERO TO ZERO

One of the Power Team members was an NFL running back before joining our ministry. He perfectly described our society's attitude toward love and acceptance:

When I scored touchdowns, everybody loved me.
But when I fumbled, I went from a hero to a zero.

In our everything-is-relative society, you are loved and accepted purely on the basis of your performance. In other words, love and acceptance are strictly conditional. Young people are told they are special only if they score higher on a test than everyone else. Athletes are honored when they score and forgotten when they don't. Girls are popular as long as they look good, wear the latest fashions, or do everything their boyfriends ask them to do. The first time they develop a blemish, can't afford the latest fad, or say no to an inappropriate sexual advance, they are dropped for the next available girl. Could that explain why so many young people feel so insecure and worthless?

God's love is not based on our performance. If it were, none of us would have a chance! We are saved by His grace through faith. That means we don't automatically deserve it. We can't earn it, achieve it, or buy it. God's love is not for sale or barter—it is free. Aren't you glad that God doesn't pick the way the world chooses? He couldn't care less about who has the most impressive résumé!

I have news for you: *Everyone*—I mean every single person on this planet—*is a five-o'clock person*. God says, "All have sinned and fall short of the glory of God" (Rom. 3:23). None of us can ever be good enough or do enough to get to heaven. Membership in God's family isn't based on anything you do. The very best of the best among us would fall a million miles short of being "good enough" to live with God on his or her own.

Some of us live better lives than others. When it comes to doing good deeds to go to heaven, that is like Olympian Carl Lewis bragging that he can out-jump me *if we're both jumping the Grand Canyon*. It is true that I can only jump about twelve feet. It is also true that Carl Lewis, who is perhaps the best human jumper in the world, can jump a full thirty-eight feet! Unfortunately, both of us would fall two miles short of reaching the other side of the Grand Canyon.

I'M GLAD GOD ISN'T LIKE US

As a charter member of the Five-O'clock People Association, I am glad that God isn't like us. He doesn't change His mind about us every time we stub our toe or fall down or fail. *God's love for us is based on His ability to love us eternally, not on anything we do.* This is the ninth key principle for living in God's favor. We have nothing to do with it once we accept Jesus. God *is* love, so He can't help Himself. He loves us because He is eternal love (1 John 4:16).

The day I asked the Lord to pick me, He healed my stuttering tongue. I haven't stuttered since I was nine. God put the broken pieces of my heart back together again, and He wrote my name in the Lamb's book of life. Best of all, He gave me what the Bible calls "the spirit of adoption" and made me a member of His family forever (Rom. 8:15).

One of the biggest complaints we hear about God's way of doing things sounds a lot like the complaints made to the landowner in Matthew 20. The workers who started working early in the morning said, "You have made them equal to us" (v. 12). They resented the fact that the last workers chosen were paid the same thing even though they only worked for a short time.

God doesn't apologize for His generosity. He gives freely to everyone who comes to Him, whether they are weak or strong, tall or short, eloquent or a stutterer. When you come to Jesus, He makes you equal in value to the leaders of countries and the presidents of the world's largest corporations. God does not play favorites.

God not only uses five-o'clock people, but He also has a plan and a purpose for every one of us:

> "For I know the plans I have for you," declares the Lord, "plans to prosper you and not to harm you, plans to give you hope and a future. Then you will call upon me and come and pray to me, and I will listen to you. You will seek me and find me when you seek me with all your heart." (Jer. 29:11–13)

Let me encourage you with a very special memory from my own life about how God let me—the boy who was always picked last—become the man who was picked first. As I mentioned in a previous chapter, when you follow your passion for God, you are going to wake up right in the middle of your destiny. If you pursue His purposes, you won't have to worry about who you will marry, where you will live, or what you will be doing ten years from now.

When I went to Bible school in Florida, God used Karl and Joyce Strader of Carpenter's Home Church to mentor me. I watched Karl lovingly restore people who had fallen. His life was the greatest lesson. Frankly, I learned more from both of them than I ever learned in Bible school. The Straders taught me how to give an altar call, how to pray, how to memorize God's Word, and how to walk with Christ day after day. God also used them to lead me to, perhaps, the greatest blessing in my life.

After the Straders returned from a pastor's conference in Spokane, Washington, Joyce told me, "We met the girl for you."

I thought, *This is crazy. I am in Lakeland, Florida, and this girl is in Spokane. We live at two opposite ends of the United States!*

When Joyce showed me a picture of this girl, I had to admit that she was attractive. Then Joyce said, "The Lord put her on my heart, and you two are meant for each other." Joyce sent some Power Team brochures to the girl's father, who was a pastor, and he asked me to hold a five-night crusade at the First Church of the Open Bible in Spokane.

The name of the pastor's daughter was, you guessed it, Ruthanne. Her father was very sympathetic to evangelists. Along with the Power Team, he had invited an evangelist who "yodeled for Jesus" and a husband-and-wife team with performing poodles (don't ask me how they linked that with God's Word).

I think Ruthanne thought I was another one of her father's sympathetic projects when she saw me—a young "muscle man" with a shiny athletic suit who breaks bricks. She probably thought, *Now I've seen it all!*

Ruthanne seemed to warm up to me when she saw her neighbor come to the crusade with his four sons. She and her family had been witnessing to this man for twenty years without success, yet they all went forward and got saved during the crusade. In fact, the church was filled to capacity with people they had never dreamed would ever come to a church meeting.

Since Ruthanne was my tour guide that week, we went out to eat together and really began to hit it off. I felt the Lord confirm that this young woman was going to be my wife. Though the Lord put it in her heart, too, Ruthanne played very hard to get.

To make a long story short, I moved to Seattle six months later. It wasn't long before I asked Ruthanne to marry me. She said no the first time I asked her, but I think God was behind that too. You see, God wanted her to choose me. I needed her to choose me. Two weeks later, Ruthanne paid me—the boy who was always picked last—the supreme compliment when *she asked me* to marry her.

She chose me. Since I am no fool, I said yes! It was then that I began to wake up in the middle of my destiny, and I really liked it. The thrill of our marriage still hasn't worn off.

TWO MEN JUMPED OUT WITH
GUNS IN THEIR HANDS

Jesus meant what He said when He declared, "With God all things are possible!"

I will never forget the five-o'clock person who walked five miles to attend a Power Team crusade in Jackson, Mississippi. He didn't have any money or a car, but he knew he needed Jesus. He got saved that night, and he was so excited about it that he actually got baptized in his clothes!

After the crusade, this man began walking back home in his wet clothes rejoicing in the Lord's blessings. Suddenly a car pulled up. Two men jumped out with guns in their hands. Both men pressed their guns to the man's head and said, "Give us your money."

He said, "I don't have any money."

The armed robbers pulled back to wipe their hands and said, "Well, why are you all wet?"

That five-o'clock man just grinned and said, "I got saved and baptized at the Power Team crusade! You know them, don't you? They are the guys who break police handcuffs, blow up hot-water bottles, crush twelve-feet walls of ice with their heads, rip in half three license plates at once, and explode four two-by-four wooden planks with their chest!"

The two gunmen looked at one another in amazement and said, "Where is this crusade being held?"

They let the man go. The armed duo was so fascinated by what their wet victim said about the Power Team crusade that they actually showed up at our meeting the very next night! They also walked forward to receive Jesus Christ as their Lord and Savior.

After the service, I heard a commotion and loud shouting coming from the sanctuary of our host church, so I went back out to the auditorium to see what was going on. Guess who was in the baptismal tank? You're right. They were baptizing the two robbers. Only God can do so much with so little!

THE POWER TEAM—ALL MEMBERS OF THE FIVE-O'CLOCK ASSOCIATION

- Keenan's father was an alcoholic. Keenan grew up with a lot of strikes against him. He grew up in a very small town with a population of 400. When Keenan was a young boy, his father spent more time in the tavern than he did at home. Keenan gained a reputation as "the boy you should avoid at all costs—he's trouble."

- Clarence's father was a Green Beret in top-flight physical condition. Clarence never dreamed that as a young boy he would have to hold his father in his arms while he died of a heart attack.

- Aaron's father used to chase his family around with a .357 magnum pistol and would shoot at the family until his gun was empty. But look at Aaron today. He's probably one of the sweetest witnesses for Jesus Christ that I know.

- Jeff Neal weighed one hundred thirty pounds in high school. Today he holds his own as a member of the Power Team, performing amazing feats of strength and boldly sharing his testimony.

- "Big James" Henderson grew up under the strong arm of a single mother with no father to guide him. This champion for Christ has a true father's heart for five-o'clock people.

- Shawn Harper ranked an unimpressive last in a class of 154. When God took hold of him, he graduated from college with a respectable grade point average and the satisfaction of proving the "experts" wrong.

- Andre Sims? Eighteen years ago he was a hoodlum, a hardened sinner with a knack for violence—until God picked him for His team.

If God can use us, just think what He can do with you? If you haven't noticed, God is trying to get your attention. Now you only have two choices: You can either say yes to Him, or you can say no. God has picked you for His team. Are you ready to do what your Coach wants you to do?

GIVE IT UP OR
LOSE IT ALL

Jennifer looked beautiful in her new prom dress. Her boyfriend enjoyed the way people looked at him in his expensive rented tuxedo. The prom was exciting for a little while, but then the couple decided they needed to add a little more to their senior prom night. They tried unsuccessfully to find someone to buy some beer for them, since they were underage and living in a dry county.

Jennifer had just about given up on the idea when she remembered something. "Look, I know where my dad has stashed a couple of bottles of whiskey. Let me sneak into the house and get them out of his closet."

While her boyfriend waited in his car, Jennifer crept quietly into the house, down the hall, and into her parents' room. Once she was sure no one was around, she opened her dad's closet and moved aside the clothing and boxes he used to cover his secret place. She found the two bottles of whiskey and cradled them in her arm while she wrote her father a note and slipped it into his secret hiding place.

Once she was sure all the clothes and boxes were back in their original position, Jennifer tucked the whiskey bottles under her arms and quietly left the house to join her anxious boyfriend, who was waiting down the street.

The couple drove away to celebrate their senior prom together with a night out on the town. They drank what was left of the entire two fifths of whiskey. On the way back home, the boyfriend was so drunk he swerved into the oncoming lane of traffic and hit another vehicle carrying an entire family. Traveling at more than sixty miles an hour, Jennifer and her boyfriend hit the car head-on. The accident left such a bloody mass of humanity on the road that word spread quickly throughout the little town.

Less than thirty minutes after the wreck, the county sheriff knocked on the front door of Jennifer's house. Her stunned father got in his car and drove to the accident scene immediately. He arrived as the paramedics covered up his daughter's mangled body. The car had been reduced to a heap of twisted metal; the smell of alcohol was everywhere.

How could this have happened? he asked himself. *How could my daughter do this?* The overwhelming shock of seeing his beautiful daughter's broken body in the bloodied prom dress, the twisted fragments of the car, and the bloody evidence of what could only have been a horrible death was more than he could take.

How would he tell his wife that their only daughter was dead? *I need something to help me get through this horrible ordeal,* he thought. *The only way I can tell my wife is to get a little something from the closet first.*

Jennifer's father somehow managed to drive his car home, and then he made his way to his closet without catching his wife's attention. With shaking hands he fumbled with the clothes and boxes that had been so carefully replaced only hours before. He was desperate to reach the liquid courage he had hidden out of sight.

Suddenly the man stopped cold when his shaking hand found

the folded note instead of the fifth of whiskey he had expected. Jennifer wrote:

Dear Daddy,

We tried to find someone to buy us beer tonight, but we couldn't find anyone. This is a special night, and we knew you had a little something hidden in the closet. Please don't be mad at us, but thanks to you, we're going to have a good time tonight.

Love,
Jennifer

This true story reminds us that the secret things we hide in the closet may be the very things that will kill our children someday. The little problem with sexual immorality on the Internet, the secret addiction to drugs or alcohol, and that small matter of unforgiveness over an offense long forgotten—you may think those things are hidden today, but tomorrow they may come back to prey on your children! *God waits for us to choose His way over our own, no matter what it costs us.* This is the essence of the tenth key principle for living in God's favor.

TWO RICH MEN CAME TO THE CROSS: ONE MAN SURRENDERED AND ONE DID NOT

Our lives can change forever with a single choice made in response to God's work in our lives. The Bible describes the responses of two prominent rich men who met Jesus Christ. One man surrendered, and one did not.

A certain ruler asked him, "Good teacher, what must I do to inherit eternal life?"

"Why do you call me good?" Jesus answered. "No one is good—except God alone. You know the commandments: 'Do not commit adultery, do not murder, do not steal, do not give false testimony, honor your father and mother.'"

"All these I have kept since I was a boy," he said.

When Jesus heard this, he said to him, "You still lack one thing. Sell everything you have and give to the poor, and you will have treasure in heaven. Then come, follow me."

When he heard this, he became very sad, because he was a man of great wealth. (Luke 18:18–23)

This young ruler was both wealthy and sincerely religious. He was also very familiar with Jewish law. When he met Jesus, he asked the most important question in the world: "What must I do to inherit eternal life?"

Have you ever wondered why Jesus said, "You know the commandments" and listed the first five commandments? I think I know the reason. Jesus knew that the number one excuse people would use to avoid surrendering their lives to Him would be, "Well, I'm really a good person. I keep the commandments, and I try to do the right thing."

Sure enough, the young ruler said, "I've kept the commandments since I was a boy." Jesus knew what this man was going to say, and He also knew what he was hiding. That is why He essentially told him, "*You still lack one thing.*"

Look closely at what He said next: "Sell everything you have and give to the poor, and you will have treasure in heaven. *Then* come, follow me" (Luke 18:22, italics mine). Jesus doesn't expect everybody to sell everything they have so they can be saved. He is trying to convey the message: "Give up anything and everything that you love and treasure *more than Me.*"

"*You still lack one thing.*" Those are sad words. Let me ask you this: "What one thing would cause *you* to walk away from the call of God?" Most of us are basically decent people. We don't commit murder, we don't steal our neighbor's groceries, and we don't abuse our children. We need to remember that being "basically decent" doesn't work with God. We also need to realize that the devil usually uses the same tactic on us that he used on this rich young man. He used *one thing* to make him miss his greatest opportunity to live in God's presence forever and accomplish great things in this life.

WHAT ONE THING WILL CAUSE
YOU TO WALK AWAY?

The Lord wasn't trying to establish a doctrine about giving up things to be truly holy. He understood the total surrender of the heart. The only way to surrender to Him is to humble yourself. Jesus was not after this man's possessions; He was after his heart.

Jesus doesn't want a lot, He wants *everything*. Then He can give it back to us with multiplied blessings! I'm not making this up. When Peter reminded Jesus that the disciples had left everything behind to follow him, Jesus said something that should encourage everyone who has ever made sacrifices to obey God's commands:

> "I tell you the truth," Jesus said to them, "no one who has left home or wife or brothers or parents or children for the sake of the kingdom of God will fail to receive many times as much in this age and, in the age to come, eternal life." (Luke 18:29–30)

That brings up the second most popular excuse God hears from people who don't want to surrender their lives to Him: I am afraid I'm going to "miss out" on something. Listen, whatever you give up for God, He has promised that He will give it back to you many times over. That could mean that if you give up the lust you've been hiding in your heart, then God may give you a great marriage where you won't need that lust anymore. If you surrender your pride, God may give you a humble heart that will produce unending joy and put a skip in your step and a smile on your face!

IT TAKES SURRENDER TO PLEASE GOD

Jesus wants the rich young ruler to surrender all. It takes more than believing to succeed at being a Christian. The Bible says even the demons believe (James 2:19). It takes *surrender* to please God and release His blessings. In all four of the Gospels and in seven other places, Jesus says that if you lose your life for Him, then you will find it. If you try to hang onto it, then you will lose it forever (Matt. 10:39, 16:25; Mark 8:35; Luke 9:24, 17:33; John 12:25). This rich man wasn't willing to pay that price, so he just walked away.

The second rich man appears in the gospel of Luke:

Jesus entered Jericho and was passing through. A man was there by the name of Zacchaeus; he was a chief tax collector and was wealthy. He wanted to see who Jesus was, but being a short man he could not, because of the crowd. So he ran ahead and climbed a sycamore-fig tree to see him, since Jesus was coming that way.

When Jesus reached the spot, he looked up and said to him, "Zacchaeus, come down immediately. I must stay at your house today." So he came down at once and welcomed him gladly. (Luke 19:1–6)

Both of these rich men were interested in Jesus, and both of them had serious questions about eternity. The difference is that this second rich man cared more about eternal things than his own reputation, wealth, or comfort. In the early 1990s the Power Team ministered to a large crowd of Australians with the same attitude.

THE POWER TEAM AND A NEW AGE CONVENTION CONVERGE

The Power Team was scheduled to conduct a weeklong crusade in the fairgrounds of a famous Australian resort town situated on the coast near the Great Barrier Reef. It was also known as a New Age haven. There were about seven churches in this town of about seventy thousand people, and most of the churches had about twenty-five members each. A larger church with about one hundred and fifty members sponsored the crusade and rented the site for the meetings.

At the same time we were conducting our crusade, there was a New Age convention! This convention also had a strong representation of people who were into witchcraft, Wicca, and crystals. We were located in the open field while the New Age convention was held in the fairground buildings, but the spiritual tension between the two factions was everywhere.

We Prayed and Nothing Happened!

About three thousand people showed up for the first night of the crusade. Right before I stood up to preach the gospel, we watched a cloud come out of nowhere and move into position right above us! Then it started to rain.

I told the Team members, "Quick, guys, do your rain-dance prayer." I wasn't asking them to perform a Native American rain dance; I was referring to our modified version of Elijah's powerful prayer of command that stopped the rain in First Kings 17:1. Every time the Power Team had prayed this prayer in previous ministry situations, the rain stopped instantly. This time we prayed, and nothing happened.

It had always worked before, but no matter how hard we prayed that night, the rain just continued to come. My first reaction was, *Uh oh, I guess I can't preach. These people have to find some shelter somewhere!* Then I noticed, to my amazement, that the three thousand attendees weren't moving. No matter how hard it rained, gushed, poured, or blew, those people refused to budge!

Then it hit me: The Lord was working an even greater miracle than stopping the rain. He had caused a crowd of three thousand *mostly unchurched people* to stay in their seats in the middle of a torrential downpour for one reason—to hear the gospel of Jesus Christ!

Fifteen Hundred People Stood Up in a Storm to Receive Christ

While the rain continued to pour down in sheets, I preached about an eight-minute message and gave the altar call. We watched in amazement when fifteen hundred people stood up in the middle of a storm in an open field to accept Jesus Christ. I guess you could say they were instantly baptized as well.

That is an amazing miracle, isn't it? What would you say if I told you *the same thing* happened *every single night for five nights?* That is exactly what happened. Day after day, thousands of Australians filed into the meetings under a beautiful sunny sky with no clouds in sight. As soon as it was time for me to present the gospel, that crazy cloud would appear out of nowhere, and the drenching rains would begin to fall. And the people refused to budge! I would pull out my soaked Bible, preach a short sermon, and watch thousands of drenched Australians take a stand for Christ!

On the last night of the crusade, seven thousand people gathered together and saw the rain cloud come just in time for the preaching of the gospel. Once again no one seemed to notice the rain. The altars were as flooded as the fairgrounds. Thousands upon thousands were saved that week.

Perhaps God responded to the hunger in the hearts of those people by pouring out His Spirit in the natural realm as well as in the spiritual realm. All I know is that God proved to me, beyond any doubt, that He can save the lost in any way He chooses and under any circumstances. He didn't want to stop the rain that week; He decided to stop the people instead. When they chose to surrender their lives to Him, He gave them eternal life in heaven and abundant life on this earth in return.

Jesus told the first rich man, "You still lack one thing. Sell everything you have and give to the poor, and you will have treasure in heaven. Then *come, follow me*" (Luke 18:22). Come follow me. Those are the three most powerful words in the whole passage.

IF GOD BELIEVES IN YOU, THAT IS ALL YOU NEED TO SUCCEED

Jesus Christ, the Son of God, is calling you to follow Him without reservation or hesitation. No one can have the same impact on the world that you can, because God has a very specific and unique purpose, plan, and destiny for your life. God knew you before you were ever born. If He believes in you, that is all you need to succeed. The problem just might be that *one thing* that you have been hanging on to. Don't be afraid you will "miss out on something."

When the first rich man walked away from his destiny, that was *the end of the story for him*. Jesus was calling him to be one of the disciples. I think God wanted to use him to change the world, but he walked away, and that was the end of his significance.

Zacchaeus, on the other hand, was also a rich man and a social

127

outcast, but he didn't hesitate. He knew he had found what he was looking for in Jesus. Christians around the world and from generation to generation can tell you the story of Zacchaeus because his life became a *significant part* of the gospel story!

What would have happened to the young rich ruler if he had said yes to the Lord? What will happen to you if you surrender every area of your life to Him? Do something significant with your life: Invest it in God!

We come into this world to fulfill a God-ordained destiny. He has invested gifts and talents in every one of us, and He expects us to use them for His glory. In the parable of the talents in Matthew 25, Jesus warns us that we will be asked to give an account for how we have invested the things God has given to us. If we put them to work, we will hear the Master say, "Well done, good and faithful servant! You have been faithful with a few things; I will put you in charge of many things. Come and share your master's happiness!" (Matt. 25:21).

Religious people like to show up on Sunday mornings, but they never get involved. They refuse to use their gifts and talents for God. They need to understand that God demands more than religious pretense and the outward appearance of surrender. God calls us to surrender all.

It takes courage to stand for God, and the proof of total surrender is that you will begin to care more about what God thinks than about the opinions of the people around you.

THEY WILL PROBABLY BOO YOU OFF THE STAGE

Brad Tuttle, one of the long-standing members of the Power Team, made a stand for Jesus many years ago, and he has never backed down. He spoke at a rough school in Chicago. The school principal warned Brad before the assembly, "These students have booed everybody off the stage for the last twenty years, and I have to warn you that they will probably boo you off the stage too. They just won't listen to you."

Brad wasn't about to back down because he had made a commitment to Jesus that he was going to keep—no matter who tried to stop him. He spoke to those students with such passion and power that when the dismissal bell rang, all two thousand students stood to their feet to give Brad a standing ovation! In fact, they refused to be dismissed until he agreed to continue speaking to them. The students finally let him end the assembly a full fifteen minutes *after* school normally ended! The school faculty said that was the greatest demonstration of God's power they had ever seen—moving the hearts of those hardened.

Once you make a commitment to Christ, you will find that your surrender doesn't mark the end of your life, only the beginning. I remember reading a story in a Bible study workbook about a stadium that was full of heroes and saints who had gathered for the biggest race of all time. The runners were lined up, the referee raised the starting gun, and the race was on. The runners exploded out of their starting blocks. Every muscle was stretched and worked to the limits of endurance as each runner strained to win the prize—all except for one runner.

When the referee fired the starting gun, this runner didn't explode from his starting position. He immediately collapsed to his knees and raised his hands in an act of surrender. When the grueling race was over and the gasping competitors had crossed the finish line, to everyone's surprise, the referee held up the hands of the lone competitor who was still on his knees at the starting blocks. He was proclaimed the winner of the race even though he had never left the starting line. How could this be?

The announcer explained to all, "The race of life doesn't go to those who strain and struggle the most, it goes to the one who surrenders to God the most."

The story of the two rich men is a story of surrender. The only way to win the prize of eternal life with Christ and abundant life on the earth is to surrender all.

The Scariest
Scripture in
the Bible

In 1989, I went on a hunting trip on Afognak Island in Alaska that pushed me to the very limits of my endurance and the brink of death. This remote island just north of the Kodiak Islands is one of the most dangerous wilderness islands in all of Alaska, but it is popular with big game hunters because of the huge Kodiak bears who roam its rugged interior. It is also home to the only herd of elk in Alaska.

Matt Crouch and I hunted together on the island each day, accompanied by a professional guide from the region.[14] It is far too dangerous to hunt on Afognak Island without a guide, but we wanted to go to a favorite spot high in the mountains on the island. The guide said he couldn't take us on that particular morning. Since we thought we knew the trail to the place, we asked if we could go by ourselves. Our guide reluctantly gave in.

We started out for the mountaintop hunting site long before morning's light and spent seven hours climbing through the mountain trails, pushing through the thick brush. We managed to reach the top of the island's mountain range and started to chase a beautiful herd of elk. Before we knew it, a thick blanket of fog set in, and we were lost. Within minutes we couldn't see more than just a few feet in front of us. The temperature plummeted from forty-five degrees to ten degrees. We knew we were in trouble because we had only prepared for moderate temperatures.

Shortly after the fog descended on us, Matt lost his .45-caliber pistol in waist-high grass and thick underbrush. Since the pistol was a gold-plated keepsake gift, we spent some time searching through the heavy brush with no success. Finally, we gave up, knowing there was virtually no chance that we would ever find it again. We knew we had two other guns with us for protection, and we had to deal with a much larger problem.

We finally decided that we had to get off that mountain right away, even if we weren't sure which direction to go in the fog. We began our descent, totally unaware that we had chosen a direction that would lead us to the wrong side of the mountain. That trail ended abruptly in a sheer cliff that dropped straight down for a half mile. We were desperately lost, and the only thing we could do was turn around and climb back up to the top of the mountain again.

Most people don't realize that when you are lost in Alaska, it's not like being lost in Texas or Virginia. If you get lost in most places, you have a very good chance of finding a road or some local residents if you keep walking in one direction. In Alaska's uninhabited wilderness, you could be lost for a month and die before you ever found another living soul.

For some reason, we found ourselves in a familiar setting once again after five exhausting hours of wandering. The fog was still so thick that we couldn't see past our own knees. Against impossible odds, we stumbled upon our original location. Matt's foot actually kicked the .45-caliber pistol he had lost earlier that day. It was an impossible occurrence, but that pistol was destined to be the key that would save our lives.

Even more hours went by as we searched frantically for a trail or path down the mountain. Finally we found a river and decided the best route off that fog-covered mountain was to follow the river to a lower elevation. Unfortunately, this was no gentle, meandering lowland river with gradually sloping banks.

Up to Our Waists in Freezing Water

We couldn't walk on the banks of the river because there weren't any. This river had "walls" that were straight up in most places, which meant we had to walk in the river itself. But we couldn't walk for more than fifteen or twenty feet without falling into the river because we were up to our waists in the freezing water, and the current was moving so swiftly that we felt as if we were "wading" through white water rapids. We knew that if we lost our footing and were swept into the main current of the river, we could only function for five minutes because of the water temperature. Ice formed all over us. Sometimes we had to clamber over jagged rocks blocking our path. Both of us took some very serious falls along the way that really weakened us.

Eventually we reached a place where the river suddenly dropped off a nearly sheer rock shelf into a treacherous waterfall. It looked too dangerous to go forward, but we knew we had come too far to go back to the mountaintop. In the end, we decided to scale the rocky cliffs around the waterfall.

I Plunged Forty Feet Straight Down into Sub-zero Water

Matt Crouch weighed 175 pounds and was a former gymnast. He managed to scale the cliff face without incident. As for me, I knew I was doomed, since I weighed in at 300 pounds at that time. I could not duplicate Matt's feat. Halfway around the waterfall, I plunged forty feet straight down into the sub-zero waters of the waterfall basin below.

133

The heavy steel barrel of the hunting rifle strapped across my back slammed into the back of my head, and when I finally came up from the swirling water, blood gushed from a deep gash there. In that moment I knew that I would die if we weren't rescued soon. The air temperature was still hovering at ten degrees. I came out of that freezing cauldron of water covered with so much ice and blood that Matt said I looked like a red Popsicle.

We were both suffering from advanced hypothermia by this time, and all I wanted to do was lie down and go to sleep. I knew that calm, sleepy sensation was a signal that I was about to freeze to death, but I really didn't care.

Matt Crouch saved my life that day because every time I wanted to sit down and give in to that hypothermic lethargy, he would scream at me, "You're not sitting down! John, I'll leave you behind. Do you hear me? You're going to be eaten by bears!"

Now this may sound silly to you, but the Kodiak bears on this island are the largest bears in existence, and they have been known to eat humans. By this time, both of our rifles had been smashed or rendered useless during our desperate descent from the mountain. In the wild, all we had for protection from the half-ton Kodiaks that roamed the island was Matt's keepsake collector's pistol.

Only moments before darkness would descend on the island, we stumbled upon the thing we had been looking for—the end of the river course. Unfortunately, we weren't standing on a beach or broad river delta. The river ended abruptly by plunging thousands of feet down to the wind-tossed waves of the bay below us. In that moment, nearly dead from overexposure, hypothermia, and crushing fatigue, we realized we had stumbled out on the *wrong* side of the mountain again! We knew that if any rescuers were still looking for us, they would probably be located on the other side of the island.

Almost at the Point of Death

We didn't know it, but every rescue boat but one had already given up the search by then, because it was almost dark. Our ability to think logically was nearly gone. To be honest, I would have given up if it hadn't been for Matt Crouch. My larger body size wasn't an asset in that situation. I'm convinced it actually made survival much more difficult for me. I wanted to go to sleep and let myself go. I knew I'd miss my wife, and I was sorry that my life would end, but an eternal sleep looked awfully good right then.

The light faded quickly, and there were only a few more minutes of daylight remaining. We were in Alaska near the Arctic Circle, and at that time of year, the sun shines continuously for up to twenty-four hours sometimes. We had probably been wandering around on that island for a good twenty to twenty-one hours at that point and just didn't have much time or life left.

We had no way to start a fire, and our bodies were already nearly dead from hypothermia. Once the night descended, we wouldn't live to see another day. As we gazed across the bay from our mountainside perch high above the water, we could just make out a tiny speck on the water in the distance. It was the last remaining rescue boat. We didn't realize it, but the rescuer literally had his hand on the engine key. He was only seconds away from starting the engines and heading for home.

Matt quickly pulled out the .45-caliber pistol he had miraculously recovered earlier that day and began to fire off rounds over and over again. In the brief time delay before the boat engine fired up, just after he had turned the key, the rescuer heard a faint pop in the distance. He quickly shut down the engine and listened for the sound again. Within moments, he headed toward our location. We fired the gun over and over again until rescue parties were able to make their way to that rocky outcropping on the side of the mountain.

On the boat trip back home, our bodies shook uncontrollably, and our teeth chattered constantly. We were unable to get out of bed for nearly three days because of the severe shock our bodies had suffered. The lesson I learned from my experience was that a journey through the Alaskan mountains is way too dangerous unless you go with a guide.

The trails of life are even more dangerous than the trails of Alaska. If you don't start every day with the Guide who knows the trails—the Lord Jesus and the Holy Spirit—then you are going to suffer needlessly and experience some painful and potentially fatal hardships and hard knocks. Every day we should begin our journey by making the Holy Spirit our guide.

Jesus Says We Need to Be Afraid!

I learned what fear tasted like during my adventure in Alaska because death was a very real possibility, and I knew it. God's Word often teaches us how to overcome the fears of this life, but there is one fear that we all need to learn. It is found in what I call "the scariest Scripture in the Bible." This fairly obscure Scripture passage records the only time in the entire Bible that Jesus says *we need to be afraid!* This passage is scarier than anything Stephen Spielberg or Stephen King could ever imagine:

> "I tell you, my friends, *do not be afraid* of those who kill the body and after that can do no more. But I will show you whom you should fear: Fear him who, after the killing of the body, has power to throw you into hell. Yes, I tell you, fear him. Are not five sparrows sold for two pennies? Yet not one of them is forgotten by God. Indeed, the very hairs of your head are all numbered. Don't be afraid; you are worth more than many sparrows." (Luke 12:4–7, italics mine)

"No Fear" bumper stickers, T-shirts, and ball caps have been popular in the United States for several years, but this saying is incorrect. It lacks the most important part of the truth about fear. The Bible says it best: "Even though I walk through the valley of the shadow of death, / I will fear no evil, for you are with me" (Ps. 23:4). You don't want to be caught in the valley of the shadow of death without God. The phrase on all of those T-shirts and ball caps should be modified to say, "No Fear—*if God is with you!*" If God is not with you, you should be terrified that your heart could stop beating any minute, because you would have to stand before a God who is bigger than the heavens and the earth, and explain to Him why you rejected the free gift of His Son's life.

My body is just a shell. I drink about twenty protein shakes a week, ride my bike, do aerobics, and work out for hours to keep in peak shape for the ministry God has given me. I take fifteen different kinds of vitamins and watch what I eat. Yet, no matter what I do, one day this body is going to go to the grave. It is just a shell, a temporary home for an eternal being.

Every person who is born into this world will one day walk through the valley of the shadow of death. I don't know about you, but it is scary to think of facing the valley of death without God.

THE ENTIRE TEAM DIED IN A PLANE CRASH

When I was attending high school in Evansville, Indiana, we lived within a mile of the University of Indiana at Evansville. Two of my friends played basketball with the college team during their freshman year. One cold and stormy winter night while I was studying, my mother came in from the grocery store and said, "I've got some very sad news, John. The entire college basketball team from Evansville went down in a plane crash, and they all were killed."

Only one player missed the plane. Dave was a redheaded guy who was the nicest guy in the world. We took some classes together before he graduated and moved on to the university. He was a great basketball player, but he didn't make the plane that day because of an injury.

Oddly enough, two weeks later, a drunk driver crossed the center line and killed Dave and his twin brother instantly. Have you ever heard the phrase: "Life is short, death is sure, sin is the cause, but Christ is the cure"? Most of the people who will die tomorrow never have any idea that today will be their last day on earth.

The young men on that college basketball team thought they were just going to play another game of basketball, but really they were flying into eternity. They never dreamed that when they boarded that plane, they were boarding their own casket.

THE WORLD'S STRONGEST MAN
COULDN'T ADD SEVEN SECONDS TO HIS LIFE

I remember the day I visited Gold's Gym in Atlanta with several members of the Power Team. That gym was like no gym I had ever seen. We saw a poster of this man on the wall that said, "The World's Strongest Man." He could actually lift more than one thousand pounds from a squatting position several times. A specially reinforced steel bar had to be constructed just to handle the massive weight this man used to lift. The ends of the bar nearly bent to the ground. This was the place where he trained.

One of the Team members said, "Man, I want to meet this guy." I felt the same way. When we asked the trainer at the gym where this man was, he said, "Well, he's not here anymore. He got into his sports car after lifting his usual one thousand pounds and drove down the street. Someone ran a stop sign and hit his car. The impact broke his neck, and he was dead in seven seconds." If the world's strongest man can't add seven seconds to his life, than neither can you.

No one but Jesus has ever defeated death, and none of us can dodge it—no matter how much money or fame we accumulate. We all have an appointment to walk through the valley of the shadow of death, and none of us can afford to be caught in that valley without God.

Jesus told us not to fear those who can only kill our bodies, but we had better be afraid of the One with the power to throw us into hell for all eternity. This was driven home to me in a way I will never forget one day when I was stuck in a traffic jam in Houston, Texas. It was on a Sunday morning at 7:30. I remember thinking how odd it was to be in a traffic jam on an interstate highway on Sunday morning.

I sat on the passenger side while the car crept along the outside lane of the highway. I rolled down my window and noticed a group of deputy sheriffs standing together talking. When I looked down, I suddenly found myself staring directly into the face of a dead man! It wasn't pretty.

His body was still lying there on the side of the road exactly as it had been found. Have you ever looked into the face of a dead person *before he was embalmed?* This man's body seemed to have a purplish-blue haze over it. His face was shrunken, and there was stiffness in his arms, hands, and fingers that appeared inhuman. Instantly it hit me: *That man is not here anymore; that's just a shell.* The man who drove our car turned to me and remarked, "He's somewhere in eternity right now." In that moment, the scariest thought came to me: *What if he had to face the valley of the shadow of death without God?*

The good news is that no one really has to. Our Creator is like the father of the prodigal son described by Jesus. This was the Lord's way of saying, "This is what My Father and your Father are like: The moment He sees you turn back toward Him, He will run to embrace you in His arms." We serve a God who has never said no to anyone who came to him with a sincere heart (John 6:37).

ARE YOU READY TO FACE THE VALLEY OF THE SHADOW OF DEATH?

Could it be possible that even this far into the book, you are not ready to face the valley of the shadow of death? I have to ask you if you're ready before I can go on to the final chapter in this book. I don't want you or anyone you love to face the valley of the shadow of death alone. I've nearly walked through that valley two times in my life. The first time was in the Alaska wilderness, and the second time happened in Africa a few years ago.

Ruthanne and I were in Africa when one of the most experienced game wardens in the area came to me and said, "Do you want to go with me to find some man-killing elephants?" I'd never been asked a question like that before, so I asked a question of my own. "What did they do?"

"Oh, they killed two villagers," he said.

"No, I meant what did the elephants do to the villagers?"

"Well, one of the elephants grabbed a woman with his trunk and beat her against some trees. All we found was a bloody stump."

"Oh," I said. "Well, what about the other one?"

"That elephant gets down on its knees and runs his tusks through people. Then he throws them up in the air and plays with them."

Don't ask me why, but I said, "Okay, I'll go with you."

I began to wonder about my sanity when the warden took me deep, deep, *deep* into the African jungle. He must have known I was having some doubts because he said, "Don't worry. If the elephants try to kill us, I'll shoot them." I believed him, of course, and that was a big mistake.

We located the elephants sooner than we expected because they had gone into a rage and killed two more villagers that day. Then we found out why. The game warden learned that a poacher had wounded one of the giant elephants. After the warden contacted his office by walkie-talkie, he told me, "I've got to go kill this elephant. If a poacher has wounded it, then it could kill a whole village full of people. Do you want to go with me?" The hunter in me answered, "Okay," before the wiser part of my brain could mount a protest.

So off we went to chase a killer elephant through the jungle. The warden explained to me that normally they do everything they can to protect the elephants in the wild. But it is a law in Africa that once a poacher or another animal wounds an elephant, he has to put it down. Elephants go into a rage when they are in pain. With their size, strength, and speed they can easily kill a whole village in a matter of minutes.

I was about to learn just how smart elephants could be. Once we sighted this giant elephant, we began to chase him down in hot pursuit. For one brief moment in the chase, the elephant dropped out of sight behind some trees. We thought it kept right on going because it was running full speed, but we didn't realize that this massive bull elephant had wheeled around behind those trees and was waiting to ambush us.

We got within fifteen feet of the thick grove of trees, where we last saw the elephant, when all of a sudden the trees literally seemed to explode! That seventeen-ton elephant charged toward us at full speed with its ears splayed out. He towered over us almost two stories high. The volume and ferocity of its angry screams just can't be described in words.

Meanwhile, the guy who bragged to me, "Don't worry. If anything tries to eat us, I'll shoot it. Just look at the size of the bullet in this gun!" had his own problems. He fired both of those big bullets at the charging elephant. One completely missed the target, and the other round hit the elephant in a way that didn't seem to faze it.

The elephant just kept coming toward us. I thought, *He shot both bullets—that's great.* The elephant was less than fifteen feet away from me and running at full speed. I had a problem: In short distances, elephants can run approximately four times faster than a man can.

I was about to relive the childhood nightmare where a monster was about to grab me, and I was so scared that my feet wouldn't move. I took off running, and then I tripped.

I thought I was a dead man. All I could do was fall flat on my face in front of thirty-four thousand pounds of angry elephant. I didn't know it then, but the game warden's second bullet had struck the elephant above the eye so it couldn't see me well enough to kill me. For that reason, the wounded elephant charged right over me without stepping on my body!

What a close brush with death! Had I died that day, I know I would have been rejoicing because I was saved. I would be in the very presence of the Lord.

HAVE NO FEAR: JESUS IS OUR BRIDGE

Are you and your loved ones ready to face the valley of the shadow of death? Above all, you need to know that your sins have been forgiven and that Jesus lives in your heart. Secondly, you should love your family and friends enough to tell them the truth about the scariest Scripture in the Bible.

As Christians, we should have no fear of the valley of the

shadow of death because Jesus is our eternal bridge over that valley. Our motto must be: "No fear because God is with me." Now, that is the good news of the gospel of Jesus Christ.

Our conviction must be to "press toward the goal for the prize of the upward call of God" (Phil. 3:14 NKJV). This is the answer to the "scariest Scripture" in the Bible, and the eleventh key principle for becoming the Ultimate Champion.

Gratefulness and Faithfulness Keep the Glory Spout Open

John Jacobs?" the man said as he came up to me in the Denver airport. "We recently attended your crusade. Let me tell you my story . . .

"I was an alcoholic, and I was dying of liver disease. At the time, I was living with my girlfriend, and my two sons just worshiped a popular heavy-metal band.

"We saw one of your Power Team posters at a grocery store, and it looked exciting and different," he said. "We decided to go to the Nichols Arena to see you in person. Then we heard you preach the gospel. That night my girlfriend, my two sons, and I walked forward and got saved."

Then he smiled and said, "That was six months ago. I have been healed of liver disease, and I haven't touched alcohol since that night. I married my girlfriend, and my two sons don't worship the heavy metal band anymore. Instead they put up Power Team posters, and they have begun to permeate their high school with the gospel."

This man was grateful for the things God had done for him. He and the members of his family had been faithful to tell others about God and what He had done for them. We need to remember that God loves to respond to such an "attitude of gratitude." That is the way you can stay under "the spout" and keep that glory pouring out.[15]

A Child's Attitude

We can learn a great deal about gratefulness from little children. When I bought a toy truck for my little boy, Trey, he immediately said, "Daddy, thank you so much! Thank you, Daddy." His gratitude just melted my heart. I can assure you that if my little boy's toy ever breaks, I won't waste any time buying him a replacement! Why? *Because he is grateful.*

The same thing happened when I took Trey to an amusement park recently. He was so overcome with joy that he said, "Thank you, Daddy. Thank you so much for taking me."

That little boy could have asked me for anything he wanted in that moment! His gratefulness just made me think, *I am so glad I took Trey to this park!* Then I realized God was using my little boy to teach me something about gratefulness. My heart just leaps for joy when my son says, "Thank you, Daddy." If my heart is fashioned after God's heart, even remotely, then God's heart must leap for joy when we thank Him and openly demonstrate our gratefulness!

The Nine Healed Lepers Still Had "Spiritual Leprosy"

God loves to bless, provide, protect, and promote us when we are thankful and grateful to Him and when we seek His kingdom and His righteousness first (Luke 6:38; Matt. 6:33). Jesus made a point of telling us about the time He healed ten lepers of their physical disease. Only one of the lepers returned to thank the Lord for healing him of an incurable disease. This revealed that the other nine lepers suffered from the much more serious "spiritual leprosy" of ungratefulness:

145

One of them, when he saw he was healed, came back, praising God in a loud voice. He threw himself at Jesus' feet and thanked him—and he was a Samaritan.

Jesus asked, "Were not all ten cleansed? Where are the other nine? Was no one found to return and give praise to God except this foreigner?" Then he said to him, "Rise and go; your faith has made you well." (Luke 17:15–19)

The spiritual disease of ungratefulness left the other nine lepers only partially healed, but the one who returned to offer thanks left the presence of the Lord totally whole, inside and out. We can learn a lot from that story.

I believe this passage reveals the biblical way to "motivate" our heavenly Father to continually open the door to His glory. Is this manipulation? Absolutely not. God sees all things, and He knows all things—including the true motivation of our hearts. When we are genuinely grateful to God for His many blessings and demonstrate it with praise, thanksgiving, and obedience, He will keep his door open, and He will guard those things He has given us. In other words, our gratefulness motivates God.

GRATEFULNESS MOVES THE HAND OF GOD

Too many churches and believers tell God what they want and need. There is a place for coming to God in humility and sharing a need—knowing He already knows our needs before we come to Him. However, I've learned that God will respond to a grateful heart much quicker than He will to a hungry heart carrying a "want list." The world—and the Church—is full of spiritually hungry people, but there are very few people on this planet who are truly grateful. Those people are blessed because gratefulness moves the hand of God.

God also used little Trey to teach me about the importance of His grace in our lives. Trey is now two and a half. He is a very normal little boy. He misbehaves sometimes; he won't always come when I call him; and it is very clear that he has a mind of his own. Even if he is working through his so-called "terrible twos" right now, it doesn't affect my love for him.

At this age, some little kids say, "No!" Trey's special phrase is, "Go away." I could be holding him on my lap or lying on the floor telling him how much I love him, when he will look at me with an ornery little smirk on his face and say, "Go away."

My first thought is that Trey is only a little boy who is just learning how to use language. His misuse of such powerful adult words at his age doesn't hurt me or rock my world! I just pray over him because I know Trey doesn't mean it.

We need to understand grace. I am an earthly father with many shortcomings, but I have enough wisdom and sense to respond with grace when my little toddler tells me to "go away."

The grace God shows toward us is so much greater that our human grace. We can't compare the two! God doesn't demand that you get saved all over again the first time you stub your toe as a Christian. He doesn't force you to "work your way back" into His good graces, and He will never disown you as a son or daughter. Our heavenly Father knows we come to Him as sinners and that we are weak in countless areas. He knows all about us, and He loves us perfectly, even though we make mistakes, disobey, and sin from time to time. He doesn't encourage us to do these things, but He *does* know we are human sinners saved by grace.

As I listened to a grateful man share what Jesus did in his life through the ministry of the Power Team, I realized once again that God has given us an important responsibility. We know who gets the glory for the good things that happen through our ministry—it goes to God and to God alone. He is the one who gave us our natural and spiritual abilities. It is God who opens doors, protects our health, enables us to minister, and perform feats of strength year after year. It is God alone who saves the souls and restores broken homes around the world.

OUR RESPONSIBILITY IS TO STAY GRATEFUL

From the men who perform the power feats on the road to the staff who support us day after day at the home office, everyone involved in the Power Team ministry is very aware that God's favor is on our ministry. Our responsibility is to stay continually grateful for God's unmerited favor, for this is the biblical way to bless and motivate our Father in heaven.

I have discovered that many people can handle failure, but only a few can handle success. I recently heard that seven out of ten men can handle failure, but only three out of ten can handle success. Many Christians tend to forget about God or take Him for granted when He begins to promote them or use their ministry in a great way. I learned a hard lesson when I was forced to apply this principle of gratitude during a hard time in my life. God used a very difficult and painful lesson in leadership to teach me how to keep His "glory spout" open through the bad times as well as the good times.

The Power Team moved to the Dallas, Texas, area in 1988, and the Lord seemed to lead me and many of the Power Team members to The North Church, pastored by Dr. Lawrence Kennedy. At the time I sensed that God was going to use him to bring godly change and guidance to my life. Sure enough, God has used Dr. Kennedy's counsel and pastoral ministry to bless the Power Team in countless ways over the years. It was during this time that I faced one of the greatest challenges of my life.

One of the newer members of the Power Team had some good leadership skills, and I had him lead some crusades in my absence. While I was out of the country, I learned that this young man had tried to recruit several of the Power Team members to help him start his own version of the Power Team. He told them that if he led the team, there would be less pressure on them as well as less travel. In other words, he tried to lure away some of the people who were dearest to me. Had these men given in, it would have devastated our ministry. He only succeeded in luring away one junior team member, and I am thankful to report that this valuable brother rejoined us several years later.

Your Reaction to Problems Today Determines Your Success Tomorrow

By God's grace, I was able to intervene in the situation, but I had to pray my way through it. My friend, you will inevitably face the challenge of dealing with people who attempt to do you wrong. The Lord showed me through this situation that our reaction to problems today will determine our success tomorrow. The Lord clearly spoke to my heart, saying, "Don't raise your hand against this man, and don't fight with him. That way, I will be free to intervene and stop him from hurting you in any way."

I am human, and I will admit that, at the time, my flesh wanted to tell the whole world what this Christian brother had done to the Power Team and me. I was irritated by the fact that his version of the Power Team posters had been reprinted with our pictures removed and new people inserted in our place—using our own printer, no less. He had also ordered uniforms, even while I thought he was leading a crusade in another city.

I learned that we all have to make choices in situations like this. We can be an Absalom, a Saul, or a David. While this man appeared to be playing the part of an Absalom, I knew I would be playing the part of an angry Saul if I publicly confronted or sued him. We would both lose, and the kingdom of God would suffer.

By God's grace, I refused to take the part of Saul. Instead of rehearsing the wrongs this man had done, I allowed God to reverse them. God is well able to close the mouths of those who criticize us if we will stick to what He has called us to do. The Power Team weathered the storm, and we did our best to keep a spirit of gratefulness as the ministry continued to grow in influence and size.

Our next great challenge had to do with handling success God's way. Through the end of the 1980s and early 1990s, we concentrated on large coliseum crusades, and hundreds of thousands came to Jesus. However, I became very concerned because so many of the new converts seemed to just disappear in the months following our crusades.

As I prayed about the problem, God reaffirmed our original vision to win the lost through "power preaching" of sound doctrine,[16] but He also spoke to my heart about a change in method. He wanted us to start ministering in local churches for three major reasons:

1. He said, "Everything I am going to do in the days ahead is through the local church."[17]

2. God made it clear we were to use our evangelistic gifts to help build the *local church*.

3. The Lord wants local churches to do what only local churches can do: to take on the extremely important task of caring for and discipling all of the people who accept Christ in evangelistic crusades.

We made the switch from large coliseums to local churches in the early 1990s and immediately began to see God's favor shower down upon us in even greater measure. This only confirmed that we had heard God's voice accurately and that His glory was blessing our obedience. We began to conduct some extremely large and successful church crusades, such as the one we held in the church pastored by Tommy Barnett. We saw nine thousand people walk forward to receive Christ during a five-night crusade!

Three Thousand Saved Despite a Seventeen-Inch Snowstorm!

Pastor Ronnie Floyd of First Baptist Church in Springdale, Arkansas, invited us to have a crusade in his church. Four thousand people packed that building every single service despite a seventeen-inch snowstorm! We even held two extra services to minister to an extra eight thousand people and saw three thousand people walk forward to give their hearts to Christ.

In 1992, Pastor Bill Purvis of the Cascade Hills Southern Baptist Church in Columbus, Georgia, asked us to conduct a crusade at his church of about three hundred fifty people. By faith, the church actually rented a football stadium, and many people were saved. They decided to have us back every eighteen months. This was a new concept to me, but at this writing we have been there six times, so far, and that church grew from three hundred fifty to five thousand members! We held our most recent crusade in their new sanctuary, which seats almost two thousand people. Pastor Purvis told me that a majority of his new converts came to the Lord during Power Team crusades! My point isn't to glorify the Power Team, but to show how God honors local church congregations that have a heart for the lost and are willing to follow up with new believers and take the Great Commission seriously. This kind of commitment is catchy. In one year alone, we tracked twelve different churches that had doubled in size because they were committed to winning the lost, and they proved it by "partnering" with the Power Team instead of merely "booking" us for a crusade.

God continued to give us a wonderful rapport with evangelical groups such as the Southern Baptist Convention, and our ministry began to grow as never before. With a broader base of ministry to the United States, we were able to reach out to other nations with great effectiveness when God opened the doors to do so. Even so, we still try to work through local churches in those nations.

The Power Team ministered in Russia in the last year before the communist regime fell from power. At least seventy-five thousand Russians packed the auditorium every night, and many came to Christ. One of the greatest miracles of the crusade was that the national television network, which was under the direct control of the communist-dominated government, broadcast our crusades across the nation as a live television special!

Only God Can Open Doors Like That

Since at that time there were only two channels for Russian viewers to choose from, it was estimated that one hundred million citizens of the former USSR (Soviet Union) watched me snap police handcuffs and preach the uncompromising gospel of Jesus Christ! Even the cameramen were getting saved! As a result of that broadcast, we believe that hundreds of thousands of people accepted Christ all across Russia. Only God can open doors like that.

We've held crusades in forty countries and ministered on television around the world. During a four-night crusade in London in 1999, nearly forty thousand people attended the meetings, and more than seven thousand accepted Christ. Our hosts told us that four hundred people stayed for an hour-long class on baptism and were baptized the Monday following the crusades. They said that, to their knowledge, it was the biggest evangelistic revival London had seen in more than fifty years.

The Power Team flew to Caracas, Venezuela, to hold a crusade in a large bull-fighting ring. The crowds just kept growing until the attendance broke all the records in the history of that nationally famous bull-fighting ring. Best of all, more than five thousand people came to know Christ while God gave us the grace to make history in that South American nation.

God instituted yet another major change in 1996 when He pointed out to me that two long-time Power Team members, Mike Hagen and Berry Hanley, had really developed as preachers. I sensed that the Lord wanted me to do what Moses had done so long before. Instead of trying to carry the load of conducting all of the crusades myself, I was to release these two outstanding men of God to lead what I call the "Power Plus" teams, under the cover of the Power Team. We still drew from the same pool of guys, but we went out in rotation. This eased the load on our families and increased our effectiveness for the Lord.

The Lord raised up even more leaders. We now have eight Power Plus crusade leaders (including myself) taking teams into more than one hundred sixty churches a year. We minister in many of America's greatest churches of all denominations, and we have thirty full-time Power Team members of all races and different Christian denominations. Some of us are Southern Baptist, some Assemblies of God, and some Nazarene, but we agree on the basics. We follow Billy Graham's ministry philosophy and stick to the Cross, leaving the teaching of the spiritual gifts to the local church.

CHUCK NORRIS WOULD LIKE TO GET TO KNOW JOHN JACOBS

It almost seemed like God opened His "glory spout" even wider in 1998 and 1999, because He began to create more opportunities to witness for Him in the national spotlight. One day the phone rang at the Power Team office. The lady on the other end of the line told our receptionist, "Chuck Norris would like to get to know John Jacobs and the Power Team."[18]

As you can imagine, I returned the call and arranged to meet Chuck at his home. After meeting a couple of times, we began to talk seriously about doing something together to help reach young people in the public schools through his "Kick Drugs out of America" program. Ultimately, Chuck invited the Power Team to be special guests on his national television program *Walker, Texas Ranger.* I couldn't believe it was happening.

Chuck Norris and his team of writers prepared a powerful script for the show that was titled "The Principle." It called for Norris to go undercover into a high school as principal to investigate a murder in the school. The Texas Ranger had the Power Team visit the school to do a positive-values assembly to counter the influence of drugs and violence.

The Power Team did feats of strength, and I spoke at three different assembly programs during the taping, which showed how kids' lives changed as a result of those messages. Of course, in the end Ranger Walker nailed the bad guy.

I have been told that millions of viewers nationally and worldwide saw the show. It was one of the first times in history that a ministry has been featured "as themselves" on a prime-time action show. That is a miracle in itself. Chuck told me that particular episode produced one of the biggest responses they have ever had.

This wonderful opportunity, and all of the others besides, were made possible solely by God's grace and power. I've learned to never underestimate the power of God. He can work through almost anything.

It is our habit to work out at local gyms wherever we go, partly to stay in shape as professional athletes, and partly to be a witness for Christ. I was training at Gold's Gym in Jackson, Mississippi, one time, when a man walked up to me and said, "I want to show you something. I thought you were going to be here today because I have seen your posters around town."

Then he pulled a rumpled Power Team flyer out of his pocket and said, "Do you see this flyer?"

I looked at it and said, "Yes," thinking *Oh, my goodness. That was printed fifteen years ago.*

He said, "I was the first one in my entire family to give my heart to Christ. It happened at this meeting, and *I came because of this flyer.*" Then he said, "I just want you to know that since that day, every relative I have has gotten saved." Never underestimate the power of God, and never hesitate to obey when He asks you to do something for Him.

A number of years ago, I was giving the altar call at the end of a Power Plus crusade in a church. The problem was that a particular woman cried so loudly that I had to stop the entire service and ask her, "Ma'am, what's wrong?"

She said, "My son was here tonight, and he left. He's not saved, and God spoke to me in a dream that his time is running out."

I looked at the people in the audience and said, "We're going to demonstrate something here tonight. We are going to demonstrate the power of the Holy Spirit to draw someone in! I don't want anyone to leave because we are going to pray." Then I prayed a special prayer the Lord gave me for bringing lost loved ones to a saving knowledge of Jesus Christ. We took biblical authority over the devil and asked the Holy Spirit to "loose the hounds of heaven" (angels) to search out this young man and draw him back in. Then we began to practice gratefulness by thanking God for His intervention.

The entire church stood and thanked God for fifteen minutes, believing that this woman's son would come back and get saved. Fifteen minutes to the moment when we began praying, the back doors flung open, and this young man walked straight down the aisle and fell onto the altar.

Afterward, he told me, "After your message, I went outside, got in my car and drove all the way home. But the last story you told about the reality of hell began to get to me so much, and I felt such a drawing that I couldn't stand it. I got back in my car and drove here as fast as I could." This is the power of the Holy Spirit.

GRATEFUL PEOPLE CAN MAKE A DIFFERENCE

Gratefulness does more than place us in a position to enjoy God's blessings and favor. It also changes us and equips us to make a real difference in the world. My friend Larry Jones, of Feed the Children, saw this in action in his own ministry. In 1979, he visited an orphanage for children with special needs in Dagoretti near Nairobi, Kenya, East Africa. Many children in this orphanage were missing arms and legs. One little boy was paralyzed from the waist down and lived in a corner of the room on a gurney. His name was Paul. Larry Jones felt he should take the time to go ask Paul, "What do you want to be for God?"

This little boy looked up at Larry with a startled expression because no one had ever asked him that question before. Even so, he *knew* the answer and immediately said, "I want to be an artist."

Larry was so moved during that visit that he paid off the mortgage for this special needs children's orphanage. He also hired an art teacher to tutor little Paul. Afterward, Larry came back to America.

Larry continued to visit Dagoretti year after year, and was surprised to find on a visit, fifteen years later, that the orphanage was filled with beautiful paintings. All of the students were in one room taking art classes. Larry couldn't get over seeing the little children without arms or legs painting pictures while holding brushes with their mouths or toes. No matter what disability each child had, each one had somehow adapted to the challenge. Do you know who was teaching the class? It was Paul. Once again, we are reminded that God can do a lot with just a little.

IT IS TIME FOR THE CHURCH TO LAUNCH OUT INTO THE DEEP

While conducting a crusade on the Hawaiian island of Molokai, I was invited to go fishing for marlin the next day. I announced at the meeting that night, "Since so many people have come forward to receive Christ, I am going fishing tomorrow. God is going to give me a *big* fish."

The next morning we went fishing with a guide who attended the local church. He told me that the water on one side of the island was much calmer, but it wasn't as good to fish in. The other side of the island was very rough because it had much bigger waves, but it also yielded much bigger fish.

I said, "Oh, I don't know. I don't think I want to go out there with the big waves. I want to go where it's calm."

We fished on the calm side of the island all day long and didn't catch anything. At the end of the day, we headed back across the channel between the two islands where the big waves were. We decided to leave our lines out during the passage. Suddenly we crossed an entire school of marlin. Until that moment, the waves were so huge that we could barely keep the lines out. I sat in the bottom of the boat wrapped in life preservers. I had one around my neck and one on each arm!

Then every one of our reels began to scream! When we hit that school of marlin, they hit our bait at full speed. Marlin like to catch their prey at high speed in high waves, and they just exploded on our fishing lines. I fought the marlin on my fishing reel for two and one-half hours while the boat cut through ten-foot swells. When we finally caught the fish with grappling hooks, we realized we had brought in a four-hundred-pound, twelve-foot-long blue marlin! The Lord had made his point. Yes, it is a lot easier to fish in the calm waters, but that is not where the big fish are.

That is exactly how we live our lives. We avoid controversy, obstacles, problems, and persecution at all costs. We like calm lives, but that is not where the big victories are. God wants His people—and His Church—to launch out into the deep. He wants us to dare to do "great exploits" for Him. That means we will have to go out and fish for people among the big waves—among the big challenges, and the big obstacles. He wants us all to become God-inspired risk takers for Him. If we aren't willing to fish where the big fish are, then we'll never see the great victories God has for us.

The very reason God has a "spout where the glory comes out" is to anoint and equip His people to spread the Good News of the gospel to a lost and dying world. He blesses the Church so the Church can be a blessing to the world. He blesses His children so they can be a light to the lost and dying around them.

I encourage you to *live life with a continual heart of gratefulness, while showing grace to everyone around you.* God will shower you with blessings and provision so you can be a beacon of life, light, and joy to the world around you. This is the twelfth key principle for becoming an Ultimate Champion.

Remember, the greatest key to the abundant life in Christ is this:

Do what you can with what you have, right where you are; then God will increase what you have, and He won't leave you where you are.

It is time to go fishing in the rough water. It's time to brave a little criticism. It's time to brave a little breaking of tradition. Most churches "fish" in the aquarium, but God says it is time to go fishing for men and women, and boys and girls, in the deep waters of the world, where a great harvest awaits us all.

NOTES

1. This name and several other names in this book have been changed to protect individuals' privacy.
2. Only a few verses later, Huldah the prophetess quoted Deuteronomy 29:25–26 in her address to King Josiah. (See 2 Kings 22:17.)
3. Based on the very *conservative* figures using only actual cases verified in 1995 by child protective services in the fifty states and the District of Columbia and reported to the National Child Abuse and Neglect Data System. The truth is that there are far more crimes committed than are ever reported. Source: U.S. Department of Health and Human Services (DHHS). Internet site: *http://www.acf.dhhs.gov/programs/cb/stats/ncands/highligh.htm*, accessed June 22, 1999.
4. ABC News Internet, Kalpana Srinivasan, Associated Press, "Lower Child Abuse Rates," April 1, 1999. Internet site: *http://abcnews.go.com/sections/living/DailyNews/child-abuse990401.html*, accessed June 25, 1999. According to the author, DHHS reports showed that the child abuse rate has hovered at or was slightly below one million in the years since 1993, when an all-time high of more than one million cases were verified by authorities.

5. National Institute on Drug Abuse (NIDA), 1996 National Household Survey on Drug Abuse, cited on Internet site: *http://www.ncadd.org/factsdir.html,* accessed June 28, 1999.

6. U.S. Department of Health and Human Services (DHHS), Centers for Disease Control and Prevention, Announcement 99146: "Cooperative Agreement for a Coordinated Community Response to Violence Among Youth," Addendum 2: Background Information and Definitions, located on the DHHS Internet site: *http://www.cdc.gov/od/pgo/funding/99146.htm,* accessed June 18, 1999.

7. Tom Curry, "Americans fret about moral decline," appearing on the "MSNBC News" Internet site: *http://www.msnbc.com/msn/283291.asp,* accessed June 24, 1999.

8. Ibid.

9. Ibid.

10. Adapted from key definitions and word derivations for the original Hebrew word transliterated as Goliath, *Golyath,* (Hebrew #1555), and its probable root term, *galah* (Hebrew #1540); supplied by James Strong, *Strong's Exhaustive Concordance of the Bible* (Peabody, MA: Hendrickson Publishers, n.d.).

11. Wiccans are Neo-Pagans who believe in magic and practice it. Unlike satanists, Wiccans claim they don't believe in the existence of God or the devil. However, they share a common disdain and dislike for the Christian belief that there is only one way to God—through Jesus Christ.

12. The number six has been called the "number of man" by many Jewish and Christian scholars, just as seven is the number that is symbolic of God. Some sources point to Revelation 13:18 as a primary biblical source for this concept.

13. When the Power Team comes to a city or region to conduct a crusade, it is our practice to go to as many high schools and

junior high schools as we can the week before the crusade begins. One or two team members go to each school to perform some power feats and speak to the student body. Although our school programs often include personal testimonies about transformed lives, we try to work cooperatively with local school officials, and we do not preach or give public altar calls at these assemblies, which explains why the young lady's public prayer to receive Christ in the high school gymnasium was so unusual. We perform some power feats to capture the attention of our audience and then follow up with a brief, fast-paced character-building message. At the end we invite the student body to attend a full-scale Power Team program held at a local church or auditorium. It is in the Power Team crusades that we deliver the gospel of Jesus Christ in all its life-changing power.

14. Matt Crouch is a longtime friend and the son of Paul and Jan Crouch, founders of the Trinity Broadcasting Network. Matt is a television producer, director, and on-air host with TBN.

15. Just for the record, I am not teaching people that there is a physical spout situated in the heavens where we can go to get our daily allotment of blessings. Nor am I saying that by "stepping under the spout where the glory comes out" we will be exempt from trials, tribulations, and difficulties in this life. God's favor shines down on us as we go through these things. This "heavenly spout" is a metaphor, a picture or earthly illustration of a greater truth used to teach us about God's giving nature and the godly character He loves to give. The biblical passages most closely associated with this concept are the "windows of heaven" in Genesis 7:11 and Malachi 3:10; the heavenly ladder or stairway seen in a dream by Jacob in Genesis 28:12; and the heavenly opening Stephen saw as he was being martyred (Acts 7:55–56).

16. By this, I mean that we use feats of strength as "bait" to fish for men. The aim of this illustrated sermon approach to evangelism has always been to clearly testify to the power of the work Jesus completed on the cross, to preach repentance, and to point to the cross in everything we do.

17. The Power Team still ministers in *coliseums when a local church (or group of churches) feels led to sponsor the outreach.* This way, all three of the Lord's guidelines are still being met.

18. Chuck Norris starred in numerous action movies, is an internationally respected martial arts champion, and is the producer and star of the long-running prime-time television drama *Walker, Texas Ranger.* He later attended our crusades and was deeply touched by the Lord's presence. Chuck currently attends The North Church in the Dallas area.

About the Author

J OHN JACOBS is an ordained Southern Baptist minister and a dedicated evangelist who reaches out to people of all ages. The founder of the world-renowned Power Team stands six feet, four inches and weighs 310 pounds. Not only is he a world-class athlete, but he is also a world-class communicator and one of the most sought-after motivational and inspirational speakers in the world.

Over the last twenty years, several million people have walked forward and accepted Jesus Christ at Power Team crusades. Jacobs and the Power Team have reached many more millions on television. In 1999 the Power Team performed its feats and ministered in more than a thousand public schools. During the past two decades, they have made free appearances in more than ten thousand schools.

The Power Team has been featured on *CNN News*, in *People* magazine, in the *Saturday Evening Post*, and on the television show *Walker, Texas Ranger*. The Power Team has grown from a single, three-man team to eight teams with thirty-one members. Jacobs's ministry has held crusades in more than eight countries, and is opening offices in England, South Africa, and Australia.

John Jacobs has a vision to reach even more lost souls with the gospel in the twenty-first century. He currently lives in the Dallas, Texas, area with his wife, Ruthanne, and their son, Trey.